WORLD WAR II

COLONIES

AND

COLONIALS

Marika Sherwood

Savannah Press

This book is dedicated to

    Peter Blackman
    Constance Cummings-John
    Cy Grant
    Ernest Marke
    Billy Strachan

Who with great patience taught me so much about the war, and much else.

Thank you!

CONTENTS

	Introduction		1
Section 1	The Immediate Pre-War Years		5
Chapter 1	Politics in the Colonies		5
Chapter 2	Politics in Britain		13
Section 2	The War		24
Chapter 3	Military Contributions by the Colonies		28
Chapter 4	Other Contributions by the Colonies		48
Section 3	The 'Home Fronts'		58
Chapter 5	The 'Home Front' in the Colonies		59
Chapter 6	The 'Home Front' in Britain		71
Section 4	International Interests in the Colonies		88
Chapter 7	American Interest in the Colonies		89
Chapter 8	The United Nations Organisation		96
Section 5	The Immediate Post-War Years		
	June 1945 – June 1948		98
Chapter 9	The Empire		101
Chapter 10	Conferences and Protests in Britain		106
	Index		115

Savannah Press © 2013 13 Church Rd, Oare, ME13 0QA, UK
www.savannahpress.co.uk   ISBN no. 978-0-9519720-7-6

Introduction

In March 1939 France and Great Britain agreed to guarantee the integrity of the borders of Poland, re-established as an independent country after WWI. When Germany invaded, Britain and France had little option but to declare war on Germany on September 3.

At that time Britain claimed about half the world as its Empire. The peoples of the colonies had been acquired/conquered from the 16th century onwards. Those who survived the conquests, and exportation from Africa as slaves, were usually deemed to be savages, who needed 'civilising' and 'Christianising'. The 'dominions' of Australia, New Zealand and Canada and then South Africa were used to settle Britain's convicts and then the surplus and impoverished population. The native peoples were almost exterminated except in South Africa.[1] Rhodesia and Kenya also became 'settler' colonies. Comprehensive statistics for emigration from the UK to the British Empire (originally including what became the USA[2]) only began to be collected in the later 19th century: about 90,000 persons per year emigrated. 'Peak emigration was reached in the last years of the 19th century and the beginning of the 20th, when over 11 million British and 7 million Irish emigrated'.[3]

The dominions were permitted a measure of self-rule: they had their own parliaments, elected by the settlers and overseen by a British governor. The colonies, and the 'protectorates' acquired after WWI,[4] were ruled by a governor

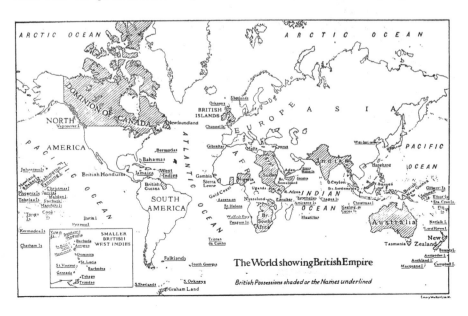

The World showing British Empire

British Possessions shaded or the Names underlined

1

(viceroy in India) appointed by Britain and usually supported by a Legislative Council of appointed Europeans/Whites. Legislative Assemblies were slowly established in some colonies. The majority of members were always White. If there were any 'native' members, they were either appointed by the governor or elected by a very limited franchise. Civil servants above the lowest level, and military officers were all White.

Our first record of the presence of peoples from Africa on the island of Britain is of African soldiers. There was an African light cavalry regiment within the Roman armies which conquered England some two thousand years ago. As no research has been carried out, our next pieces of evidence are from the Scottish royal records in 1205 and from the illustration of an African in the 1241 'Abbreviatio' of the Domesday Book (a form of census, carried out in 1086).

Records then jump to the Tudor period from when there is a considerable amount of written and painted evidence.[5]

While the peoples of the Indian subcontinent were never seen as quite as 'uncivilised' as the peoples of Africa, or, for example, the Aborigines of Australia, racist attitudes were well engendered in the colonies and in Britain. Margery Perham, Oxford historian and advisor to the Colonial Office in 1942 recalled that

at school I had absorbed the idea that pre-European Africa was a place of complete and anarchic savagery.... [Whites in Britain] regard[ed] other races of men almost as if they were another species.[6]

The exigencies of war had necessitated the use of colonial manpower during World War I (as it had in previous wars of conquest).[7] The need arose again in World War II. Manpower in uniform was needed on all battle fronts, also in the shipyards and on merchant ships, and in the mines, plantations, farms, and factories producing war materials for Britain. They were also required for the construction of army, navy and air bases in the colonies.

1241 'Abbreviatio' of the Domesday Book

This small book in only an introduction to the manifold contributions of the colonies to the war. The focus is on the countries of origin of much of Britain's 'Ethnic Minority' population today – that is, on India, Africa and the 'West Indies', and includes some indications of life in these colonies. Thus there is no mention at all, for example, of Malaya or Ceylon, and hardly any of the dominions. There is also a focus on Britain, as it controlled the colonies, and had a large resident 'Black' population.

The book is divided into a number of sections, to make it easier for readers to find the information most important to them. Section 1 introduces the situation in the colonies and of 'Black' peoples in Britain immediately prior to the outbreak of war. It is impossible, of course, to even glimpse all the colonies, or all Britain, and all the 'situations'. So the 'stories' I relate are only examples.

Section 2 outlines the many types of contributions to the war by the colonies, military and other. Given the vast amount of foodstuffs and raw materials, including oil, that came from the colonies, as well as the funds and manpower, one has to begin to wonder if the war could have been won by Britain without the colonies.

Section 3 deals with the 'Home Front' – living condition, and working conditions, shortages, mistreatment. Many historians have written about the Home Front in the UK, without mentioning the Black population.[8] Apparently there was no 'Home Front' in the colonies which needed describing. But there *was* a 'Home Front' in the colonies, and I outline at least some of the war-time conditions there.

Section 4 is on international interests in the colonies, focussing on that of the United States. It then offers a glimpse of colonial issues at the founding of the United Nations. Finally Section 5 outlines the post-war issues in the colonies and the political struggles by Black Britons in the immediate post-war years.

There are copious footnotes at the end of each chapter, giving not only the sources of information, but suggestions for further reading. Sometimes some further relevant information is added.

— — —

NOTES

There is currently an ongoing debate about the use of the term 'Black' – should we use 'African'? In the 1960s and 1970s, 'Black' included peoples from the Indian sub-continent. Today the term 'Asian' is used for them.

1 There were almost no native survivors on the islands the British called the 'West Indies'.

2 Between two and two and a half million Britons were living in the USA by 1790.

3 W.A. Carrothers, *Emigration from the British Isles*, (1929) London: Frank Cass, 1965, Appendix 2. Data from www.migrationwatchuk.org/pdfs/6_2_ Emigration_from_the_uk.pdf suggests 'a net emigration of between 5000 - 7000 people per year from the 16th to the end of the 18th century'. See, eg., G.F. Plant, *Overseas Settlement*, OUP, 1951; Douglas Hill (ed), *Great Emigrations* series, London: Gentry Books, 1972-3. There was no accurate data kept on the emigration of Britons and Irish prior to 1853. From then till 1912 about 11 million emigrated. About 3 million emigrated between 1911 and 1939. (W.H. Carrier & J.R. Jeffrey, *External Migration*, HMSO, 1953) Many millions of pounds were spent on assisted emigration. For example, Plant estimated that £4.5 million was spent on assisted passages up to 1873. (p.40)
As indicated, not all emigration was voluntary: for example, indigent women and children were 'exported' in the 19th century to Australia and Canada. On these aspects, see, eg. Gillian Wagner, *Children of the Empire*, London: Weidenfeld & Nicolson, 1982; Philip Bean & Joy Melville, *Lost Children of the Empire*, London: Unwin Hyman, 1989; Don Jordan & Michael Walsh, *White Cargo*, Edinburgh: Mainstream Publishing, 2008. See also review by Robert Houston of M. Harper, *Adventures and Exiles*, in the *BBC History Magazine*, May 2003, p.57.

4 A 'protectorate' was a colony handed over to the victorious by the vanquished powers after WWI, as a 'protectorate' ie, to rule.

5 See Marika Sherwood, 'Black People in Tudor England', *History Today*, October 2003 and 'Blacks in Tudor England', BASA *Newsletter*, #38 Jan. 2004. #39 April 2004 & #40, Sept. 2004; Onyeka, 'The Missing Tudors: Black People in 16-century England', *BBC History Magazine*, 13/7, July 2012, pp. 32-33. (On this era there is one completed and one PhD dissertation in progress.) The major text on the history of 'Black' peoples in Britain is Peter Fryer, *Staying Power*, London: Pluto Press, 1984.

6 Perham in *The Times*, 14/3/1942, quoted by K.L. Little, *Negroes in Britain*, London: Kegan Paul, 1947, pp. 221, 224. This is, as far as I know, the second book to look at Black Britons, and the racial prejudices they were experiencing. The first, Eric J. Dingwall's *Racial Pride and Prejudice* was published in 1946.

7 On West Indians in WWI, see eg., Glenford Howe, *Race, War and Nationalism: A Social History of West Indians in the First World War*, Kingston: Ian Randle, 2002; Humphrey Metzgen & John Graham, *Caribbean Wars Untold*, University of the West Indies Press, 2007, chapter 9; Richard Smith, *Jamaican Volunteers in the First World War*, Manchester University Press, 2004.

8 Stephen Bourne, *Mother Country - Britain's Black Community on the Home Front 1939-45*, London: The History Press, 2010.

SECTION 1

THE IMMEDIATE PRE-WAR YEARS

This section gives a glimpse of the social and political situation in a few of the colonies. Though not as severe as in the United States, a 'colour bar' operated in all colonies. This meant that jobs in the civil service and in most private companies above the lowest level were reserved for Whites. Trade was mostly in the hands of Whites, as was all shipping. Living areas were unofficially segregated and there was almost no social intercourse between the ruling class and the ruled. Workers, usually very badly paid and with no rights, were beginning to protest about their conditions in some colonies.[1]

Most often there was only primary education - for a small proportion of the children. It was often provided by missionaries, but received some financial support from the government. Infrastructural development was exclusively to enable the cheapest and fastest transport of raw materials to the ports for export.

Racial discrimination was also profound in the UK. In some cities, for example Liverpool and Cardiff, the Black population was concentrated in one part of the city. In many cities there were Black organisations, struggling against discrimination and providing support for each other.

CHAPTER 1

POLITICS IN THE COLONIES

When war broke out, the British government was much concerned about the colonies. Why was the government so concerned? The colonies were anything but peaceful. Would they support the 'Mother Country'? Would they succumb to temptations by Britain's enemies? Would the 'agitators' use this opportunity to press for equality, for accountability by their British overlords, and even demand greater freedoms – or even independence?

The Colonial Office (CO) noted that 'it was essential to convince coloured people that their assistance is needed and valued. It is a matter of first political importance to effect this... The West Indian Governors have indicated that the formation of military units was very desirable on political grounds.' However, the Foreign Office informed its Consuls that 'only offers of service from white English speaking British subjects should be considered'. The colonial Governors were advised that 'it is not desired that non-European British subjects should come here for enlistment'.[2]

THE WEST INDIES

From the mid-1930s onwards workers throughout the West Indies were striking, marching and protesting about their wages and conditions of work. There were also marches by the unemployed. *The Times* reported on 7 February 1939 that the

> Riots in Jamaica hampered trade and industry and unemployment presented a grave problem. Strikes occurred in British Guiana and Trinidad sugar industries and on the Trinidad oilfields. Landslides did much damage in St.Lucia. (p.38)

Demonstrations were dealt with very harshly. To give just two examples: in Trinidad and Jamaica, between 1935 and 1940, 47 demonstrators were killed and over a thousand arrested by the governments.[3] Alexander Bustamente, the leader of the striking sugar workers in Jamaica, was arrested twice. His lawyers managed to obtain his release. Uriah Butler, the main labour leader in Trinidad, was not so fortunate. Sentenced to 2 years hard labour for 'invoking' a strike in 1937, he then spent all the war years in prison, as the UK feared that he would incite oil workers to strike.[4] Britain sent marines to occupy the island. Trinidad was crucial to the war effort as it was the largest oil producer in the British Empire, supplying about half the needs of the Royal Navy and the RAF.[5]

Alexander Bustamente

On all the islands strikers were put down with the aid of imported British military. In Britain many supportive meetings were organised – for example, there was one sponsored by the International African Service Bureau (IASB) in Trafalgar Square on 26 June 1938. (F.A. Ridley, then a member of the Independent Labour Party, was the only non-IASB speaker.) Immediate amnesty was demanded for the strike leaders imprisoned in Trinidad and Barbados. The government announced that it was setting up a commission to investigate conditions in the West Indies. The IASB, the League of Coloured Peoples (LCP) and the Negro Welfare Association (NWA) and other organisations protested about the exclusion of any <u>colonial representatives</u> from the commission. They sent a joint 'Memorandum' to the government with broad-ranging

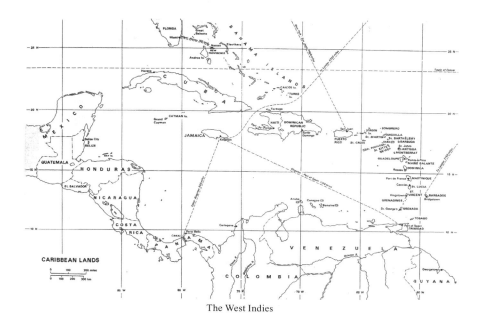

The West Indies

recommendations, including agricultural, education and health issues.[6]

The Commission, led by Lord Moyne, began its investigations almost immediately. The first recommendations were announced in 1940. These included improving wages and employment conditions, and increasing 'native' representation in the colonial governments. Some were implemented towards the end of the war. However, the full *Report, West India Royal Commission, presented by the Secretary of State for the Colonies to Parliament* was not published until June 1945. We can only presume that Commission's findings were believed to be too damaging to Britain's reputation for publication during the War.

THE GOLD COAST AND NIGERIA

There was residential segregation, not only in 'white settler' colonies such as Kenya, Rhodesia and South Africa, but also in Accra (Gold Coast, now Ghana) and Lagos (Nigeria) and other large cities in the African colonies. Fearing disturbances, during 1941-43 the Colonial Office discussed the levels of segregation in the West African colonies, but decided not to make any changes.[7]

In the Gold Coast cocoa farmers began withholding their produce from monopolistic 'combines'

Uriah Butler, escorted to jail

7

formed by the British exporters in 1937. They offered £20 per ton now, whereas the previous year the farmers could sell for £35 per ton.[8] *The Tribune* reported on 23/11/1937 that three million cocoa workers were on strike. Probably more accurately the *Chicago Defender* on 2 April wrote of 'hundreds of thousands of native farmers' being on strike, and that the IASB was pushing for a commission to investigate the situation. Not very surprisingly the Gold Coast Governor banned the importation of the IASB's news-sheet, *Africa and the World*. (The *Negro Worker*, the ITUC-NW's journal, was already banned.) George Padmore, who had edited the *Worker* and now edited the *World*, managed to get his parliamentary supporters to question this in Parliament in June 1938. The government could not 'interfere', the Colonial Secretary maintained.[9]

Men with the appropriate educational qualifications began to demand that they should be accepted as eligible for the Administrative service in the colonial government in Nigeria and the Gold Coast. Their request was considered – and refused by both the governors and the Colonial Office.[10]

In Accra, to prevent qualified African pilots volunteering for the RAF, European members of the multi-racial flying club closed it down and formed another club, for Whites only.[11]

Sierra Leone

In 1937, after training as a teacher in England for some years, Constance Cummings-John[12] returned to Freetown.

The extent of repressive legislation existing there was noted in the London newspaper, *New Times & Ethiopian News* on 24 June 1939 (pp. 3,5,6). In London she had been an active member of the LCP, of WASU, and then of the IASB. Within months of her return, and now the principal of the African Methodist Episcopal Industrial School, she established a branch of the LCP. In the LCP's monthly journal, *The Keys*, she reported on 6 February 1938 (pp. 6-7) that civil servants had been forbidden to join the LCP, or the West African Youth League recently founded by I.T.A. Wallace-Johnson, or any other organisation. Another issue she raised was the unequal pay for Africans and Europeans with university education joining

Constance Cummings-John,
speaking in Freetown

the civil service: the commencing annual salary for an African was £45 and for a Europeans £400.

In 1939 the police arrested Wallace-Johnson[13] and searched his home, but found 'no evidence that he intended carrying out any seditious act'. The 2,000 copies of the *African Sentinel* (the re-named IASB news-sheet) in his possession were confiscated under the Sedition Ordinance.[14] He was released and then re-arrested, as the Governor declared that he could 'arrest anyone who, in his opinion, is likely to prejudice "safety and defense" if permitted his liberty'.[15] Wallace-Johnson was put on trial without a jury and received a 12-month prison sentence. In fact he was not released from prison until 1944.

More very restrictive Acts were soon passed, copying some passed in South Africa. These empowered the government to deport anyone 'whose presence is considered undesirable', to prohibit the importation of any 'undesirable' literature, and to punish/imprison anyone deemed to be committing 'seditious acts'.[16] Nevertheless, about 7,000 participated in a protest march in October 1938 regarding wages which were so low that workers could not feed their families. They asked for the Governor to be recalled.[17]

SOUTH AFRICA

By 1911 Europeans settlers formed 20% of the population.[18] They 'took over' all the high-yielding, fertile land. Thus in order to pay the taxes imposed on them Africans were forced to work for the European settlers for miniscule wages. They could not rise above the lowest level, whether they worked on farms, in mines, or elsewhere. Workers were forbidden to strike. (Twenty had been killed in a strike in 1920 in Port Elizabeth.) South Africa was divided into four 'provinces' and it was only in Cape Town that a very few Africans had the right to vote for a European to represent them in parliament.

Segregation was total. Access to schools was grossly limited. In 1938 a Bill extended segregation to the 'coloured' community – that is, the often 'mixed' descendants of Africans/Malays/Indians/Javanese/Europeans.[19] The African National Congress, formed in 1923, attempted to fight against all the imposed restrictions.

There were also new issues regarding South Africa: General Smuts, soon to become Prime Minister, had announced that he wanted to annex Bechuanaland, Basutoland and Swaziland. The *Manchester Guardian* printed a letter from the IASB on 26/4/1938 stating that 'the natives of the protectorates are hostile' to this takeover. The IASB called a protest meeting in Trafalgar Square on the 8th of May.[20]

India

The 1939 Defence of India Act gave the Viceroy of India the power to pass any ordinance (law) which he considered necessary for the 'security' of India and

Jawaharlal Nehru

for the 'proper' prosecution of the war. The Indian National Congress, led by Jawaharlal Nehru,[21] was outraged by the Act and other Emergency Ordinances. Then, without any consultation, the Viceroy declared that India was at war. This naturally led to further rage. The Congress condemned fascism, and declared its neutrality. It asked Britain to declare its war aims regarding democracy and imperialism. And demanded independence.

Initially the Congress Party refused to co-operate in the war effort. This attitude altered when Japan entered the war and conquered Singapore in February 1942. (The colony had been garrisoned mainly by Indians and Australians.) Congress now agreed to support the war.

Mohandas Gandhi[22] demanded immediate independence and with the support of the Congress Party launched the Quit India movement. All the Congress Party leaders and tens of thousands of others (estimates are 60,000 – 100,000) were imprisoned.

The Muslim League (the other major political organisation in India) was also pro-independence, but opposed the mainly Hindu-led Congress on many issues. Led by Muhammad Ali Jinnah, the League wanted autonomy for Muslims. Nevertheless, the League announced its support for Britain for the duration of the War.[23]

Whether there should be Indian officers in the large (and historically often used for imperial conquests) Indian Army, was discussed for decades. Eventually

Muhammad Ali Jinnah & Mohandas Gandhi

a college was set up to train officers, but only for appointment to the few battalions which were being 'Indianized'. Twenty-eight had graduated in 1938. That an Indian officer should ever attain a superior status to a White officer (or even to Whites in the ranks) was absolutely unthinkable. The 'cantonment clubs' of White residents, including military officers, operated a colour bar.[24]

NOTES

'TNA' refers to The National Archives, in Kew, London.

Hansard is the official report of the proceedings of both Houses of Parliament. The name 'Hansard' was officially adopted in 1943 in honour of Luke Hansard (1752 - 1828) who was the printer of the *House of Commons Journal* from 1774. References are always to a column ('c'), not a page number. All *Hansard* quotations are from House of Commons debates.

1   For a summary of the situations in the colonies, see eg. Barbara Bush, *Imperialism, Race and Resistance*, London: Routledge, 1999.
    George Padmore wrote for many African-American newspapers, (eg. *Chicago Defender*), which were willing to print information banned or ignored in Britain.
2   TNA: CO 363/1673 (6364), 1939, undated 'Official CO Notes'; FO to Consuls, 10/11/1939; CO to Governors, 24/12/1939.
3   Sarah Britton, '"Come and See the Empire by the All Red Route!": Anti-Imperialism and Exhibitions in Interwar Britain', *History Workshop Journal*, #69, 2010, pp.68-89.
4   Butler was released after an MP in London questioned his ongoing detention in April 1945. (*Hansard*, 11/4/1945, vol.409, c. 1831) Butler had served in the West India Regiment in WWI. See, eg., Richard Hart, *Labour Rebellions of the 1930s in the British Caribbean Region Colonies*, Caribbean Labour Solidarity and the Socialist History Society, 2002, now available on www.socialisthistorysociety. co.uk/hart.htm
5   Scott B. MacDonald, *Trinidad & Tobago: Democracy and Development in the Caribbean*, New York: Praeger, 1986, pp. 57, 60, 63.
6   *New York Amsterdam News*, 16/7/1938, p.4; *Chicago Defender*, 23/7/1938, p.24, 20/8/1938, p.24 & 1/10/1938, p.24; TNA: CO 295/599/70297, Part 2.
7   TNA: CO96/774/11. According to the *Blue Books* (annual reports from each colony) for Kenya (1938) and the Gold Coast (1939), there were c.15,000 Europeans resident in Kenya and c.3,000 in the Gold Coast.
8   *New Statesman & Nation*, 9/4/1938, pp.664-5; *West Africa*, 5/2/1938, p.127.
9   *New York Amsterdam News*, 25/6/1938; *Philadelphia Tribune*, 30/6/1938; George Padmore (henceforth 'GP'), 'Exclude West Indians from Commission', *Chicago Defender*, 20/7/1938, p.24.
10 John Flint, 'Scandal at the Bristol Hotel', *Jnl. of Imperial and Commonwealth History*, 12/1, October 1983, p.80.
11 *West Africa*, 3/2/1940.
12 See LaRay Denzer, *Constance Agatha Cummings-John*, Ibadan: Humanities Research Centre, 1995; obituaries in *Guardian*, 2/3/2000 and *Times*, 14/3/2000; entry in Hakim Adi & Marika Sherwood, *Pan-African History: Political Figures from Africa and the Diaspora Since 1787*, London: Routledge, 2003, pp.29-33.

13 Wallace-Johnson was constantly challenging the colonial authorities of Sierra Leone, Nigeria and the Gold Coast. In 1935 with Nigerian activist Nnamdi Azikiwe then also in the Gold Coast, he formed the West African Youth League which became a very active political organisation. He worked with and received much support from George Padmore. On the confiscation, see *West Africa*, 26/11/1938, p.1499. For a brief summary of his life, see entry in Adi & Sherwood (2003 – n.12), pp.185-189. See also LaRay Denzer, 'ITA Wallace-Johnson and the West African Youth League', *Int. Jnl. of African Historical Studies*, 1973, 6/3, pp.413-452 & 6/4, pp.565-601 and 'Wallace-Johnson and the Sierra Leone Labor Crisis of 1939', *African Studies Review*, 1982, 25/2-3, pp.159–183.

14 This was questioned in Parliament, as reported by GP in *The New York Amsterdam News*, 25/6/1938, p.11, and *Philadelphia Tribune*, 30/6/1938.

15 GP, 'British Seize African Youth Leader', *Chicago Defender*, 2/12/1939, p.1.

16 *Voice of Ethiopia*, 1/7/1939, p.1; *New Times & Ethiopian News*, 1/7/1939, p.8.

17 *West Africa*, 29/10/1938.

18 'Coloureds' formed 8% and Asians 2.5% of the population in 1911, and also in 1951. Africans were a consistent 67%. Whether the censuses were correct is debatable. Data from Alex Hepple, *South Africa*, New York: Frederick A Praeger, 1958, p.261. For a more recent comprehensive history, see T.R.H. Davernport, *South Africa*, London: Macmillan, 1991. See also H.J. & R.E. Simons, *Class and Colour in South Africa 1850-1950*, Harmondsworth: Penguin Books, 1969.

19 Malays, Javanese and Indians had been imported as slaves by the early Dutch settlers. From 1860 Indians were imported by the British as farm labourers.

20 *Chicago Defender*, 8/5/1938, p.24; *New Times & Ethiopian News*, 30/4/1938; *Barbados Observer*, 18/6/1938.

21 There are many many books on Nehru. See, eg., *Jawaharlal Nehru, An Autobiography*, New Delhi: Jawaharlal Nehru Memorial Fund & OUP, 1936; S. Gopal, *Jawaharlal Nehru*, London: Jonathan Cape 1975; A. Gorev & v. Zimyanin, *Jawaharlal Nehru*, Moscow: Progress Publishers, 1982.

22 Also many books on Gandhi. See eg., M.K. Gandhi, *An Autobiography*, (1927) Harmondsworth: Penguin Books, 1982; R.M. Gray & Manilal C. Parekh, *Mahatma Gandhi: an essay in appreciation*, Calcutta: Associated Press, 1924 & London: Student Christian Movement, 1925; Judith M. Brown, *Gandhi: Prisoner of Hope*, New Haven: Yale University Press, 1989; Tariq Ali, *The Nehrus and the Gandhis: an Indian Dynasty*, London: Picador, 1985.

23 See Lawrence James, *Raj: The Making and Unmaking of British India*, New York: St.Martin's Press 1997, pp.539-41; *Left*, October 1939.

24 David Omissi, *The Sepoy and The Raj*, London: Macmillan Press, 1994, especially chapter 5, 'Indian Officers and Indianization'.

CHAPTER 2

POLITICS IN BRITAIN

BLACK/AFRICAN AND INDIAN POLITICAL ORGANISATIONS

Apart from local associations focussing more on their local issues, there were a number of very active national Black/African and Indian political organisations in Britain in the late 1930s. Not all can be reported here.[1] Their concerns varied as did their political stance, veering from the communist-oriented Negro Welfare Association (NWA) to the more conservative League of Coloured Peoples (LCP)[2] and the more radical West African Students Union (WASU)[3] and International African Service Bureau (IASB).[4] The India League focussed exclusively on India.

The **LCP**, had been founded in 1931 by the Jamaica-born British-trained physician Harold Moody. It attracted a mainly professional membership, including White philanthropists concerned with racial issues. The LCP worked with local organisations on racial/social issues in Britain and lobbied MPs and the government on these and colonial matters. The League published a

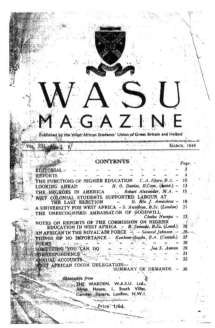

monthly journal, *The Keys*, renamed *Newsletter* in 1939. During the war all publications had to be very careful, as they could be charged with sedition if they were 'too' critical of the British government.

WASU had been established by Nigerian Ladipo Solanke and Hubert Bankole-Bright of Nigeria/Sierra Leone in 1925. It functioned as a hostel, a social and educational centre and as a campaigning organisation; it also published a journal, *Wasu*, somewhat intermittently. (It must be emphasised that most students from West (or East) Africa were adults; many came to Britain to study after years of working at various occupations in their home and sometimes in neighbouring colonies/countries. Some also came with experience of political activism at home. There were no universities and very few high schools in the colonies.) WASU convened meetings, conferences and campaigned on all issues regarding Africa.

The **IASB** was the successor to the International African Friends of Abyssinia, established to protest about the Italian invasion of Abyssinia (Ethiopia) in 1935. The founders/activists were West Indians George Padmore,[5] C. L. R. James,[6] Ras T. Makonnen,[7] Chris Braithwaite (a seaman who used the name 'Jones')[8]; Sierra Leonean I. T. A. Wallace-Johnson[9] and Jomo Kenyatta[10] from Kenya. The Bureau published newspapers, pamphlets, held weekly meetings in Hyde Park and protest gatherings in Trafalgar Square. Both the IASB and WASU used all possible means to influence parliament.[11]

The **Negro Welfare Association (NWA)** was established by Arnold Ward, a seaman from Barbados who had settled in England after being interned

George Padmore

by Germany in WWI. Linked with the International Trade Union Committee of Negro Workers, a communist-led organisation, it campaigned against imperialism and capitalist exploitations, and for colonial independence. As the other organisations, the NWA maintained contact with activists in the colonies and supported any who came to Britain to approach the government/parliament.[12]

The **India League**, originally called Home Rule for India League, was founded in 1912. Under the leadership of Krishna Menon from 1930, it campaigned for India's independence. It held meetings around the UK and Menon also spoke at conferences organised by others. Menon wanted to interest Britons of all classes in the struggle against the injustices imposed by colonial rule and in the struggles for independence. The League's Parliamentary Committee lobbied other MPs and the government.[13] Menon was elected as a councillor to the London Borough of St.Pancras 1934 – 1947 and was briefly a Labour Parliamentary candidate in Scotland.[14]

Both colonial issues and those affecting African/Indian/Black Britons were taken up consistently by these organisations, sometimes in co-operation with each other and also with White-led societies such as the Independent Labour Party (ILP), the League Against Imperialism (LAI), and to a lesser extent with the Communist Party and the Fabian Colonial Bureau.[15] The national organisations also worked with the local associations, attending their meetings and campaigning on international, national and local issues.

Ras T. Makonnen

'Coloured' Seamen[16]

Overseas trade was the 'backbone' of Britain's wealth and 'superiority'. This needed a vast merchant navy and hence tens of thousands of merchant seamen. Given that conditions on board ships used not to be the best, often not enough Whites applied, so men had to be recruited more broadly. The Navigation Act of 1660 permitted the employment of seamen from 'his majesty's … plantations'; a few years later this was extended to 'mariners from the King's Possessions in Africa, Asia and America'. As these men were 'cheap labour', they were very popular with the shipping companies. The National Union of Seamen did not consider pressing for the equalisation of wages for Whites and Blacks/Colonials. It attempted to prevent their employment, for example by demanding bribes at the docks when seamen were being recruited.[17]

It is impossible to obtain accurate figures for the makeup of the merchant navy, or even the total numbers employed at any time. According to the 1938 Census, 159,313 men were 'employed on British sea-trading vessels'; 45,182 were from the 'British Commonwealth', of whom about 20,000 were Lascars (ie, from India) and about 6,500 were Africans and West Indians. But as these are Census figures, they do not take into account men not in port.[18]

Wages for 'coloured', including Lascar seamen, doing the same work as their White shipmates were always lower; they usually also had less living space on board ship and received less to eat. For example, in 1938 Black seamen from Liverpool were paid £6.10.0 (£6.50) per month while a White seaman doing the same work was paid £9.10.0 (£9.50); those recruited in Africa were paid even less. African seamen were often employed on vessels on which Whites refused to work.[19]

RACIAL DISCRIMINATION

Newspapers such as *The Keys* and the IASB's papers regularly reported on the day-to-day instances of racial discrimination faced by the local Black populations and by Black visitors. Even servicemen returning to their colonial homes after WWI reported that they had faced what they called 'negro hatred' in England.[20]

The Colonial Office (CO) noted in April 1939 that some West African students who had tried to enlist had been 'rebuffed' and that at Cambridge University 'blacks' had not been allowed to join the Officer Training Corps. A meeting was held at the CO to discuss 'Defence: employment of non-Europeans': it was 'appreciated that the employment of large batches of coloured men would give rise to difficulties'.[21] That there was racial discrimination against 'coloured men' in the local defence services, such as the Air Raid Precaution Service (ARP), was reported by George Padmore in an article in the *Chicago Defender* of 21 October 1939.

It was announced on 19 October 1939 that 'non-pure Europeans' would be eligible for temporary commissions in the military during the war. However,

Mr Lees of the Colonial Office advised his colleagues that 'this does not, of course mean that British subjects who are obviously men of colour will in practice receive commissions…only that the men will not be turned down on "Pure European descent" basis at the recruitment offices'. Another internal memo stated that 'we only need skilled men…commissions will be from ranks except for those with flying qualifications'.[22] Thus the public announcement was a camouflage for retaining the colour bar. As a Foreign Office memorandum stated in February 1944, 'we must keep up the fiction of there being no colour bar while actually only those with special qualifications are likely to be accepted'.[23]

In its December 1939 *Newsletter* the LCP noted that no commissions had been given out since the announcement.

POLITICAL ACTIVITIES

Some of the major conferences/events relevant to these issues were:

1938

There was a '**Peace and Empire**' conference in Glasgow in January 1938. It was probably organised by the ILP and the NWA. About 500 attended, according to the brief report in *The Keys*. Padmore argued that:

> imperialism was as much a capitalist tyranny as fascism… In a war, colonial people should be encouraged to revolt against their capitalist / imperialist rulers… Complete independence must be demanded… He called upon the British Government to institute democracy in one of their colonies as an earnest of their genuine anxiety in this matter.[24]

There was also a Peace and Empire conference in London on 15 and 16 July, arranged by the India League and the London Federation of Peace Councils. Jawaharlal Nehru of the Congress of India was one of the speakers.[25]

The militant Socialist International's **Anti-Imperialist Congress** was held on 'Empire Day', 24 May. The accompanying exhibition showed:

> what an interesting story can be told of anti-imperialism with a little care… George Padmore told of conditions in West Indies and South Africa, and pointed out that only by their actions would the British workers show their solidarity with the colonial masses… The general tone of the discussion proved that the audience was in favour of rendering every support to the colonial people in their struggle for self-determination.[26]

Also in May the six-month long **British Empire Exhibition** opened in Glasgow. It was supported by aristocrats and industrialists. The local United Socialist movement under Guy Aldred called for it to be boycotted.[27] For three weeks in August 1938 the ILP and the IASB mounted a counter-exhibition. Called the **Workers' Exhibition**, it aimed to educate visitors about the realities of working conditions and the vast array of hardships imposed on colonial peoples by Britain.[28] Their pamphlet, *Come and See the Empire by the All Red Route* took its readers on a tour of the Empire, pointing out the horrors along the way. It noted that the ILP was 'the only political party putting up an uncompromising struggle against Imperialism'. The exhibition was formally opened by Ethel Mannin, a socialist member of the ILP, who gave some examples of conditions in some of the colonies. She noted that the 'prejudices of the imperialist mentality are probably the most powerful in the world because they are backed by interests of self-preservation'. The exhibition and the pamphlet aimed to counteract the misinformation being purveyed and listed the 'main firms operating within the Empire [who were] the real owners of this large slice of the globe'. Jawaharlal Nehru, then leader of the Indian independence movement, sent a message of 'utmost support'. In January 1939 the exhibition was also mounted in Friends' House in London.[29]

The **Scottish Peace Council** called its own conference in September 1938. About 600 attended. The ILP representatives argued that 'in a war colonial people should be encouraged to revolt against their capitalist / imperialist rulers', and demanded complete independence.[30] But that, of course, was far from the intentions of the government or of the British Empire Exhibition in Glasgow.

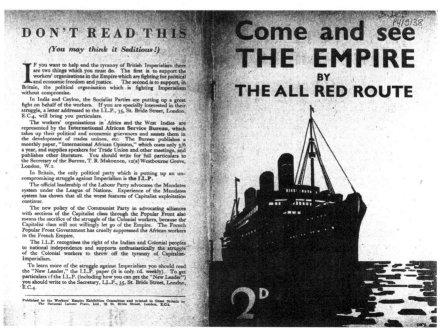

Late in 1938 the **International African Service Bureau** issued a manifesto:

> Brothers of Africa and of African descent... We denounce the whole gang of European robbers and enslavers of the Colonial peoples – all are the same, IMPERIALIST EXPLOITERS... While we deplore a war and the ruin it will cause, Europe's difficulty is Africa's opportunity. Blacks everywhere, under whatever flag, in war and in peace, know but one goal – INDEPENDENCE – and we summon our brothers everywhere not to be caught by the lying promises the Imperialists make. We call upon you to organise yourselves and be ready to seize the opportunity when it comes.[31]

1939 – PRE-WAR

In January 1939 the IASB was the co-sponsor of a conference with Fenner Brockway of the ILP. J.H. Hudson of the ILP argued that the 'British Empire was the greatest threat to peace … The emancipation of subject peoples is an essential condition for full democracy at home'. One result was the formation of the **British Centre Against Imperialism** which was to be led by a council of 19, comprising 10 colonials and 9 'imperialists'. A similar organisation was set up in France. The two organisations issued 'A Warning to Colonial People' in August 1939:

> The colonial masses in war, as in peace, can have only one aim, one goal – INDEPENDENCE. And we summon you in whatever country – India, Ceylon, Burma, Palestine, Africa – all people who fight for this end, to unite against the warmongers, both Democratic and Fascist, and all those who at this hour pledge in your name your living in defence of

the Imperialists... We denounce the whole gang of European robbers and enslavers of the colonial peoples... all are the same IMPERIALIST BANDITS whose common aim is the enslavement of humanity through-out the world.[32]

The ***Conference of African Peoples, Democracy and World Peace***, organised by the LCP, the NWA, the Gold Coast Students Union and the Coloured Film Artists Association was held on 7-9 July 1939. Apart from representatives of these organisations, Arthur Creech Jones (future Labour Colonial Secretary), and W. Mainwaring MP (an ex-miner), were among the speakers. Princess Tsahai of Abyssinia shared the platform with Krishna Menon of the India League; the opening speech was by Peter Blackman of the NWA. The issues discussed were oppressions in India; 'self-determination for people in Africa and of African descent'; the need for trade unions in the colonies; repressive legislations in the colonies preventing free speech; and social/economic conditions in the Caribbean. Padmore and Makonnen of the IASB stressed the need to actively struggle to achieve self-determination. Sir Stafford Cripps (recently expelled from the Labour Party for advocating co-operation with communists in the approaching war) argued that this 'cannot be an immediate, practical

Peter Blackman (in the 1980's)

political possibility'. Harold Moody of the LCP believed that a 'strong Africa' could only be achieved by co-operation with Europeans. R. S. Nimbkar of the All-India Trade Union Congress called for the unity of all exploited people whether 'black, white or yellow'. W. Ofori Atta,[33] Peter Blackman and a number of speakers emphasised the ignorance, misconceptions and lack of interest in the colonies in Britain.

About 250 people attended and approved a number of resolutions. The Conference pledged itself to 'secure the following demands for the people of Africa and the West Indies':

1. Universal adult suffrage
2. Universal, free, compulsory education
3. Freedom of speech, press and organisation
4. Full rights for political, trade union, co-operative and peasant organisations, and a minimum level of labour and social legislation
5. Immediate abrogation of all existing repressive legislation.[34]

NOTES

1   For the most comprehensive history of people of African origins/descent in the UK, see Peter Fryer, *Staying Power*, London: Pluto Press 1984. On **Cardiff**, see eg, Neil C. Sinclair, *The Tiger Bay Story*, Cardiff: Butetown History Project,1993; Marika Sherwood, 'Racism and Resistance: Cardiff in the 1930s and '40s', *Llafur (Welsh Labour History Journal)*, September 1991 and Alan Llwyd, *Black Wales*, Cardiff: Gwasg Dinefwr Press, 2005. On **Liverpool**, see eg, Andrea Murphy, *From Empire to Rialto: Racism and Reaction in Liverpool 1918-1948*, Birkenhead: Liver Press, 1995; Marika Sherwood, *Pastor Daniels Ekarte and the African Churches Mission*, Savannah Press, London 1994 and Ray Costello, *Black Liverpool: The Early History of Britain's Oldest Black Community 1730-1918*, Liverpool: Picton Press, 2001. On Yemenis, Adenese and Somalis in **South Shields**, see Richard L. Lawless, *From Ta'iss to Tyneside*, University of Exeter Press, 1995. Not all research is on major ports. See, eg, Louisa Adjoa Parker, *Dorset's Hidden Histories*, Poole: DEED, 2007. Some local organisations are now also researching, for example there is ongoing research in **Northampton** and **Birmingham**. See eg, Barbara Willis-Brown and David Callaghan (eds), *Black people in the West Midlands 1650-1918*, Birmingham, SCAWDI, 2010. (Scawdi is the Sparkbrook Caribbean and African Women's Development Initiative.)

2   On Dr Harold Moody and the LCP, see David A. Vaughan, *Negro Victory: The life story of Dr Harold Moody*, London: Independent Press, 1950; Roderick Macdonald, 'Dr Harold Arundel Moody and the League of Coloured Peoples, 1931-1947, *Race*, 14/3, 1973, pp.291-310; David Killingray, *Race, faith and politics: Harold Moody and the League of Coloured Peoples*, London: Goldsmiths College, 1999.

3   On WASU, see Hakim Adi, *West Africans in Britain 1900 – 1960*, London: Lawrence & Wishart 1998; and also www.wasuproject.org.uk. Many African students in the UK who were active WASU members, eg, Kenyatta and Nkrumah, led independence movements on their return home.

4   The IASB was one of, if not *the* founding organisation of the Pan-African Federation and called the 1945 Pan-African Conference. See H. Adi & M. Sherwood, *The 1945 Manchester Pan-African Congress Revisited*, London: New Beacon, 1995. See also eg, Jonathan Derrick, *Africa's Agitators*, London: Hurst, 2008; Fitzroy Baptiste & Rupert Lewis (eds), *George Padmore*, Kingston: Ian Randle, 2009.

5   The sole biography of Padmore, by J.R. Hooker (*Black Revolutionary: George Padmore's Path from Communism to Pan-Africanism*, New York: Praeger, 1967) is inadequate. (I hope L.E. James' PhD on him will be published.) See Fitzroy Baptiste & Rupert Lewis (2009 – n.4) and entry in Hakim Adi & Marika Sherwood, *Pan-African History: Political figures from Africa and the Diaspora since 1787*, London: Taylor & Francis, 2003. During the war Padmore wrote for many African-American newspapers, (eg, *Chicago Defender*), which printed information banned or ignored in Britain.

6   See John La Guerre, *The Social and Political Thought of the Colonial Intelligentsia*, Mona: ISER, 1982; James D. Young, *The World of C.L.R. James*, Glasgow: Clydeside Press, 1999; Paul Buhle, *C.L.R. James: The Artist as Revolutionary*, London: Verso, 1988; and entry in Adi & Sherwood (2003 – no.5).

7   There are no biographies of Makonnen, born George Griffith in British Guiana. But see Kenneth King (ed), *Pan-Africanism from Within*, Nairobi: OUP, 1973, and entry in Adi & Sherwood (2003 – no.5).

8   See Christian Høgsbjerg, 'Mariner, renegade and castaway: Chris Braithwaite, seamen's organiser and Pan-Africanist', *Race & Class*, 53/3, January–March 2012, pp.36-57.

9   On Wallace-Johnson, see fn13, Chapter 1.

10 See James Murray Brown, *Kenyatta*, London: Fontana, 1974 and Jomo Kenyatta, *Facing Mt. Kenya*, London: Secker & Warburg, 1938.

11 There is, as yet, no full account of the IASB, but see the memoirs of Ras T. Makonnen, a central figure, in King (1973 – n.7), chapters 8 – 12.

12 Another Barbadian, Peter Blackman, took over the leadership of the NWA in the late 1930s. See my entry on him in the *Dictionary of National Biography*, OUP, 2012. There are no histories of the NWA currently available, but there is a chapter on it in Hakim Adi's forthcoming book, *Pan-Africanism and Communism: the Communist International, Africa and the Diaspora, 1919-1939* (Africa World Press, 2013).

13 On the League, see K.C. Arora, *Indian Nationalist Movement in Britain* (1930 – 1949), New Delhi: M C Mittal, 1992. On Indians in Britain, see Rozina Visram, *Asians in Britain: 400 Years of History*, London: Pluto Press, 2002.

14 Marika Sherwood, 'Krishna Menon, Parliamentary Labour Party Candidate for Dundee 1939-1940', *Scottish Labour History*, vol.42, 2007. See also T.J.S. George, *Krishna Menon*, London: Jonathan Cape, 1964.

15 See, eg, Susan D. Pennybacker, *From Scottsboro to Munich: race and political culture in 1930s Britain*, Princeton University Press, 2009; Stephen Howe, *Anticolonialism in British Politics*, Oxford: Clarendon Press, 1993; Arthur Creech Jones (ed), *New Fabian Colonial Essays*, London: Hogarth Press, 1959.

16 On some of the early history, see Alan Cobley, 'Black West Indian Seamen in the British Merchant Marine in the Mid-nineteenth Century', *History Workshop Journal*, 58, 2004, pp.259-274.

17 Marika Sherwood, 'Race, Nationality and employment among Lascar seamen, 1660 to 1945', *New Community*, 17/2, 1991, pp.229-244. There was a regular column, 'Seamen's Notes' by Chris Jones in the IASB's *International African Opinion* 1938-39.

18 R. Hope, *A New History of British Shipping*, London; John Murray, 1990, p.383. The figure for African/West Indian seamen is for 1937, from Jack Woddis, *Under the Red Duster*, London: Senior Press, c.1947, p.84. He states that the wages, etc for 'coloured' seamen was about 40% of that of White seamen in the same positions. (p.86) See also Laura Tabili, *"We Ask for British Justice": Workers and*

Racial Difference in Late Imperial Britain, Ithaca: Cornell University Press, 1994.

19 *Empire*, July 1938; Sherwood (1991 – n.17), p.241.

20 Trinidad *Argos*, 18/7/1919.

21 TNA: CO 323/1669; also CO 323/1692/2 & /4.

22 *LCP Newsletter*, November 1939; TNA: CO 323/1673 (63641A), Internal Memorandum by Lees, 26/9/1939; CO 363/1673 (6364/1), Internal memo, 11/10/1939; Churchill to CO, 16/10/1939.

23 TNA: FO 371/43005, quoted in Marika Sherwood, *Many Struggles: West Indian Workers and Service Personnel in Britain (1939-1945)*, London: Karia Press, 1985, p.53.

24 *The Keys*, 6/2/1938, p.15; *New Leader*, 30/3/1938, p.7; *Controversy*, February 1938; Padmore also contributed to an ILP Lecture Course that year, speaking on 'Imperialism and War'.

25 *Left News*, July 1938.

26 *Chicago Defender*, 16/7/1938.

27 Glasgow City Library: 'Boycott Bellahouston', B.E.Leaflet #6, February 8, 1938.

28 Sarah Britton, '"Come and See the Empire by the All Red Route!"': Anti-Imperialism and Exhibitions in Interwar Britain', *History Workshop Journal*, #69, 2010, pp.68-89. *The Glasgow Herald*, June – September 1938: the paper estimated that about 1.2 million people had visited the main exhibition. It also noted on 16 May that the Shop Assistants Union was about to approach the organisers regarding the long working hours and inadequate wages of the workers there. See also Bob Crampsey, *The Empire Exhibition of 1938: the Last Durbar*, Edinburgh: Mainstream Publishing, 1988.

29 'Empire with the lid off', *Forward*, 13/8/1938, p.6; 'Slums of Empire', *Forward*, 20/8/1938.

30 *International African Opinion¸* October 1938, p.14; *Forward*, 1/10/1938; *New Leader*, 30/9/1938, p.7.

31 *International African Opinion¸* October 1938, p.9; *Controversy*, October 1938.

32 *Forward*, 28/1/1939; Derrick (2008 – n.4), p.421.

33 Prior to his enstoolment as Omanhene (Chief/King) of Akyem Abuakwa in Eastern Gold Coast in 1912 Nana Ofori Atta was a civil servant in the colonial administration. He was in Britain to oppose some of the 'obnoxious' laws passed to deal with the cocoa holdup/strike. ('Enstoolment' means 'coronation', not by being crowned but by sitting on the sacred stool.)

34 *New Times & Ethiopia News*, 8/7/1939, pp.6, 15; *West Africa*, 22/7/1939, pp.986-7; *Colonial Information Bulletin*, 15/7/1939.

SECTION 2

THE WAR

World War II began on 9 September 1939. But, apart from wanting to conquer Europe, Hitler had another interest. Germany had declared that 'the colonial demand is comprised for us today in two words – Bread and Honour... Germany has no interest in a mandate, but demands for her own that which rightly belongs to her before God and man.'[1] That is, Germany wanted to reclaim Tanganyika, South-West Africa, Togoland and the Cameroons, which had been put under 'mandate' after Germany lost WWI. Italy declared war on Britain and France on 10 June, 1940 and allied with Germany. In 1935 Italy had invaded and taken over Abyssinia (Ethiopia), the colony it had lost after WWI. Italy was also the colonial master of Eritrea, much of Somalia and Libya. France also had many colonies in Africa: would they accept Vichy rule (ie, government of France which collaborated with the Axis powers once Germany had invaded France), or follow Charles De Gaulle, the leader of Free French Force opposed to the Axis? All German troops and the government of Germany surrendered on May 8, 1945.

Japan joined the war on December 7, 1941 by bombing the US fleet anchored in Pearl Harbour, Hawaii. It wanted to prevent the U.S. Pacific Fleet from inter-

Gerald Bell, first 'Black Canadian' joined the Canadian Air Force in 1931. During the war he trained bomber pilots in Yorkshire, England.

fering with its plan to extend its empire, which had begun in 1937 with the invasion of Manchuria (China). Its dedicated troops conquered much of East Asia and then turned towards India. They were stopped mainly by Indian and African troops. On August 6 and 9 1945 the USA dropped atomic bombs on the cities of Hiroshima and Nagasaki. About a quarter of a million people died. Japan surrendered on 15 August 1945.

The British refused to use troops from Africa or the Caribbean to point the gun at Europeans. This did not apply to Indians, who were used in Italy and were instrumental in the taking of Monte Cassino, crucial to the conquest of Italy by the Allies. (The French had no such racial problems, recruiting about 120,000 men in their colonies in Africa; many fought in France and 16,000 were taken prisoner by the invading Germans.[2])

It is, of course, absolutely impossible to give a full account of what the colonial troops achieved on the many war fronts. The ubiquitous colour bar prevented colonials rising in the ranks until late in the war. Many were not fighting troops but labour corps, given the official title of 'Pioneer Corps'. They carried stores, equipment and ammunition; built roads, harbours, airports, bridges; carried the wounded on stretchers; later they drove and repaired vehicles of all kinds. Some recruits to the military, whether fighting or labour corps, were volunteers. Others were conscripted.

Chapter 3 outlines the military contributions and chapter 4 the vast array of other contributions from the colonies. There was so much from so many sources. So, again, just few examples are given.

Researcher Stephen Bourne has found some Black Britons who served in the war: five served in the RAF: Percy Gale and Arthur Young, both from Cardiff and Londoner Vivian Florent, who all died during the war; two more Londoners, both musicians, Ray Ellington and Reginald Forsythe were in the RAF. Another musician Leslie Thompson, Jamaica-born but London resident, served in the Royal Artillery. Yorkshireman Geoff Love served in the King's Royal Rifle Corps. Another Londoner, Cyril Charles Alcindor, joined the 2nd Bedfordshire and Hertfordshire Regiment in the 1930s; he was raised to the rank of Lieutenant in 1944, then promoted to captain after the war, but died of pneumonia in 1946.

Three women have been chronicled. Lilian Bader of Liverpool, accepted and then discharged by the NAAFI because of her colour, then served briefly in the Women's Auxiliary Air Force. Londoner Amelia King was turned down by the Women's Land Army until questions were asked in Parliament. The one woman known to have served in the military is Noor Inayat Khan, who had been accept-

Te Moananui-a-Kiwa Ngarimu VC   Noor Inayat Khan   Flight Sergeant Leonard Waters

ed by the Women's Auxiliary Air Force in 1940. She was recruited by the Special Operations Executive in late 1942 and trained as a secret agent / radio operator as she was a fluent French speaker. Flown to France, from June 1943 until her betrayal, she worked with the resistance networks. When captured and tortured, she refused to divulge any information. She was shot dead in the Dachau concentration camp on 13 September 1944. In November 2012 a commemorative statue to her was erected in London's Gordon Square – financed not by the government but by private supporters.[3]

On the practice of the 'colour bar' by the military, see chapter 6.

The role of the indigenous populations of the 'dominions' of Australia, New Zealand and Canada are not detailed in the following chapters. Very briefly: in 1941 Australia formed the fully segregated Torres Strait Regiment and accepted some Aborigines as volunteers into its military. Flight Sergeant Leonard Waters was the first and only Aboriginal fighter pilot.[4]

West Africa reported on 2 March 1940 that there were 150 of 'African descent' in the Canadian Expeditionary Force which had just arrived in the UK. As it was not till 1942 that Canada began to accept some of the 'indigenous population' into its military, it is likely that many of these men were West Indians. As there was no recruitment in the Caribbean, many had gone to Canada to volunteer.[5]

Gerald Bell, first 'Black Canadian' joined the Canadian Air Force in 1931. During the war he trained bomber pilots in Yorkshire, England.[6]

In New Zealand, what became the 28th (Maori) Battalion was raised in 1940 as part of the Second New Zealand Expeditionary Force. Nearly 16,000 Maori enlisted. Initially under White officers, they served in the Greek, North African and Italian campaigns. Maori Platoon Leader Te Moananui-a-Kiwa Ngarimu was awarded the Victoria Cross in 1943 posthumously: he had died while attacking a major German fort in Tunisia on 27 March 1943. Corporal Sefanaia Sukanaivalu, who was also awarded the VC posthumously, served with the Fiji Military Forces, a part of the New Zealand Army. He had died under Japanese fire on 23 June 1944, at Bougainville (Maldives) when attempting to rescue his comrades.

The question we have to ask: could Britain have won the war without all these colonial contributions?

Sefanaia Sukanaivalu, VC

NOTES

1   'Voice of Africa' by George Padmore, *News Chronicle*, 14/12/1938.
2   On this history, see eg., Tony Chafer, 'Forgotten Soldiers', History Today, November 2008; M. Echenberg, '"Morts Pour la France": The African soldier in France During the Second World War', *Jnl. of African History*, 26/4, 1985, pp.363-380; Gregory Mann, Native Sons: West African Veterans and France, Durham, NC: Duke University Press, 2006; Paul Anderson & Angus Calder, *Time to Kill: the soldiers experiences of War in the West, 1939-1945*, London: Pimlico, 1997. Only about half of those in the German POW camps survived. David Killingray, 'African voices from two world wars', *Historical Research*, 74/186, November 2001, pp.425-443; quote is from p.438.
3   Stephen Bourne, *The Motherland Calls: Britain's Black Servicemen, & Women 1939-1945*, Stroud: The History Press, 2012; email from Jeff Green re Alcindor, 23/11/2012; www.findagrave.com/cgi-bin/fg.cgi?page=gr&GRid=49145645.
4   It must be noted that Aborigines were then not 'citizens' of Australia. See, eg www.skwirk.com.au/.../australia...world-war.../different-perspectives-...:
5   On Black Canadian troops in WWI, see Calvin W. Ruck, *The Black Battalion 1916-1920: Canada's Best Kept Secret*, Halifax: Nimbus Publishing, 1987.
6   *Akili*, November 1994, pp.1, 3.

CHAPTER 3

MILITARY CONTRIBUTIONS BY THE COLONIES

Soon after the war broke out, the British government began to discuss the possibility of using military recruited in the colonies – after all, they had been used in the First World War. The governors were not enthusiastic. The War Office wanted labourers only. Mr Lees of the Colonial Office (CO) advised that in the West Indies, 'it should be possible to raise some units, which, while nominally military… would actually be employed on duties somewhat analogous to those performed by labour battalions'.[1]

Recruiting centre in Accra, 20 November 1943

There was much propaganda in the colonies about the need to support the 'Mother Country', as it was feared that the refusal of volunteers by the military might evoke disloyalty. That Britain was playing the central role in the war, and not the USA or the USSR, was to be emphasised; and that it was not a 'white man's war', but a 'war of civilisation'.[2]

Very reluctantly in June 1940 the **RAF** (but not its Middle East Command) lifted its colour bar and some Africans, Indians and West Indians were recruited to be trained as flying crew.[3] (Most applicants were rejected on medical grounds.) Some won awards: for example, Nigerian Akin Shenbanjo was awarded the Distinguished Flying Medal in 1944 and Sierra Leonean Ade Hyde the Distinguished Flying Cross in June 1945.[4] Despite the success of these men, from May 1944 there was a long debate among government departments about re-imposing the colour bar. To avoid negative publicity, the Air Ministry agreed in mid-1945 that 'on paper coloured troops (would) be eligible for entry....but the process of selection (would) eliminate them'.[5]

Thus the exigencies of war overcame racial prejudices – to some extent.[6] In 1941 it was decided to use African troops as labourers in North Africa and the Middle East; by 1942 necessity compelled the use of combatant African troops – but not in Europe.

CONDITIONS OF SERVICE

African soldiers were the lowest paid, Indians received a little more and White Britons much more. (This was a similar hierarchy to that for merchant seamen.) Officers, with very few exceptions, remained White. A large, but unknown proportion of the African and Indian 'troops' were in fact 'pioneer corps' that is, doing menial tasks such as carrying equipment and building roads.

The 'pyramid' within African troops put White South Africans at the top: they were paid 72 shillings per month, with West Africans and then East Africans, paid a maximum

THE BARBADOS OBSERVER

Government Notice

Recruitment For Training As Ground Staff In The R.A.F

LIABILITY OF SERVICE

ENLISTMENT of Candidates for service in connection with the above mentioned scheme is now open to volunteer. Recruits will be enlisted into the Royal Air Force for the duration of the present emergency, and may be required to serve in any part of the world. Selected applicants will be put on a waiting list and will only be enrolled when definite transport arrangements have been made.

CONDITIONS

(a) Applicants must be between the ages of 18 and 32 inclusive.
(b) Standard minimum height—5 feet.
(c) Applicants must be able to assimilate training, but need not necessarily have had secondary education.
(d) Applicants will be required to pass a Medical examination.
(e) Family Allowance will be payable in respect of the wife and children of married recruits. No other allowances will be paid. Suitable men will be selected for training in R.A.F. trades. Until trained they will be paid at Group V rates and then at the rate appropriate to the trade.

TRADES REQUIRED

Men are urgently needed for engineering, woodworking, wireless, electrical, clerical and storekeeping trades.

Prior to enlistment candidates considered suitable will be interviewed by a local selection board to decide the trade in which they will be trained.

RATES OF PAY

Selected candidates will be enlisted in the 'classification' Aircraftman 2nd Class ('AC 2') Thereafter promotion up to Leading Aircraftman ('LAC') depends upon technical ability and farther promotion upon power of leadership

RATES OF PAY—AIRMEN—A C 2 to CPL
(INCLUSIVE) PER DAY

Rank	Group I	Group II	Group III	Group IV	Group V including unskilled
A C 2	4s 9d	4s 6d	4s	4s 3d	3s
A C 1	5s 6d	5s 3d	4s 9d	5s	4s 6d
L A C	6s 6d	6s 3d	5s 3d	5s 6d	5s
C P L	8s 6d	7s 6d	6s	6s 6d	5s 6d

FAMILY ALLOWANCE

Subject to the airman making an allotment from his pay of 6d a day when receiving 3s a day, and 1s when receiving a higher rate, an allowance varying with the number of children will be paid to his wife Any extra amount the airman wishes to contribute from his pay can be included.

HOW TO APPLY

Applications must in the first instance be made in the candidates own writing to the Labour Commissioner, stating their date of birth and standard of education

Barbados Observer, 20 November 1943

of 26 shillings, at the bottom. Food historian Lizzie Collingham relates that 'British soldiers in the Indian Army got much more generous weekly rations than the Indian troops who got no meat, or vegetables or milk'.[7]

Africans also had to contend with segregation. For example, Bildad Kaggia, a Kenyan serving in the King's African Rifles (KAR), in Egypt reported that

in my unit there were five different messes: the officers' mess, which was only for Europeans as there were no African officers; European sergeants' mess; African sergeants' mess; European privates' mess and African privates' mess.

The practice of racial hierarchy was endemic: for example, African Non-Commissioned Officers (NCOs) had to 'both salute and defer to European NCOs with whom they served in the colonial forces'.[8]

West Indian troops faced slightly less discrimination than Africans. Lt. Col. Whitehorne of the Caribbean Regiment reported that

in Egypt our troop's pay books were endorsed "BOR", ie "British Other Ranks", whereas the African troops were referred to as "AOR", ie "African Other Ranks", so our troops could enter places in Egypt that denied entry to African troops.[9]

The files I saw in the Tanzanian archives many years ago give details of pay scales: Africans received a maximum of 26.2% of the pay of Whites of the same rank.[10] The ubiquitous discrimination resulted in a polite letter of protest to the authorities in 1943 by Africans serving in the Middle East. Responding to the consequent investigation, the Resident in Buganda replied that 'It seems to me that the points raised amount more or less to exact equality of treatment both as regards food, amenities, pay, liquor and general freedom of movement for all persons without discrimination of race, who are doing the same type of work. I have not myself a great deal of sympathy for the demands put forward.'[11] There were no moves towards equality by the British government.

There was a similar gap in the 'War Service Gratuities': the British private with a basic pay of three shillings per day, received a gratuity of ten shillings per month. The figures for East Africans in the KAR were one shilling per for day and three shillings and sixpence per month.[12] In East Africa a 'war gratuity' for each month of service was paid on discharge. The son of an injured veteran from Rhodesia claimed recently that all his father ever received was a £10 gratuity. The maximum paid to an African was half that given a

King's African Rifles

White soldier. In many colonies savings schemes were introduced in the hope that the men would save enough to support their families and to have some means of survival when discharged.[13]

Africans were entitled to four weeks' **annual leave**, but were seldom granted this. As explained by Captain D.H. Barber, 'there were not enough African leave camps to permit this... So during the first three years an African was lucky if he got as much as one week's leave a year'.[14]

Whether all disabled discharged men were paid a pension, and if so how much has not been possible to ascertain with any validity. David Killingray's recent work appears to indicate that payments varied from colony to colony and that only the very seriously disabled received pensions – in *some* colonies. He also suggests that once colonies became independent, they were expected to assume the payment of pensions. If men serving in labour corps who became disabled received pensions – or indeed their conditions of service and pay rates - has been impossible to discover.[15]

Hansard, HC Debate 24 January 1945 vol 407 cc814
NATIVE SERVICE PERSONNEL (PENSIONS)
Captain Prescott asked the Secretary of State for the Colonies (1) whether pensions are paid to the native rank and file of the King's African Rifles who are discharged as unfit for service on account of war wounds; and, if so, at what rates; (2) whether pensions are paid to natives recruited under the Compulsory Service Ordinance in East Africa for the Eastern African Military Labour Corps, Pioneer Corps and Signals, who have been discharged as unfit for service on account of war wounds; and, if so, at what rates.
Colonel Stanley Disability awards are payable at common rates for all the units he has mentioned. For full details I refer him to the memorandum entitled "Colonial Troops (Pay, Allowances and Pensions)," a copy of which was sent to the House of Commons Library on 28th August, 1943.
Captain Prescott Is it not a fact that the payments are in the form of a gratuity, and not by way of pension, and that, therefore, recipients who spend their gratuities have nothing of a permanent nature to compensate them for their war injuries?
Colonel Stanley No, Sir, that is not the fact. Normally, they can get both disability pensions and disability gratuities. It is only where the degree of disablement is less than 20 per cent., that they are paid only gratuities.
Sir W. Wakefield Will the right hon. Gentleman consider issuing or making a statement about plans for rehabilitation?
Colonel Stanley That is rather a different question, and I should be glad if the hon. Member would put it down.

AWARDS AND DEATHS

One publication lists 'colonials' being awarded a total of 35 Distinguished Service Orders (DSO), 180 Military Crosses, 56 Distinguished Conduct Medals (DCM) and 300 Military Medals (MM). Of these, the men in the

KAR and the Royal West African Frontier Force (RWAFF) were awarded 8 DCMs, 74 Military Medals, 133 Mentions in Despatches, and 22 Certificates of Gallantry.[16] In the RAF, Jamaican John Ebanks was awarded the Distinguished Flying Medal and Trinidadian Ulric Cross the Distinguished Service Order and also the Distinguished Flying Cross.[17]

On 1 May 1943 German bombers sank the **ss *Erinpura*** carrying troops from Alexandria to Malta. Among those killed were 633 Basotho (or 'Basuto') soldiers of the African Auxiliary Pioneer Corps and 54 Indian seamen. In 1944 the **ss *Khedive Ismail*** was sunk by the Japanese on its way to Bombay from East Africa: 1,297 were killed, including 996 officers (presumably Whites) and men (presumably Africans) of the East African Artillery's 301st Field Regiment.[18]

Hansard HC Debate 29 November 1945 vol 416 cc1735								
CASUALTIES TO ALL RANKS OF THE ARMED FORCES OF THE BRITISH COMMONWEALTH AND EMPIRE REPORTED FROM 3RD SEPTEMBER, 1939, TO THE END OF THE WAR								
	United Kingdom[1]	Canada	Australia	New Zealand	South Africa	India	Colonies	Total
Killed, including died of wounds or injuries	244,723	37.476	23.365	10,033	6,840	24.338	6,877	353,652
Missing	53,039	1.843	6,030	2,129	1,841	11.754	14,208	90,844
Wounded[2]	277,090	53.174	39.803	19,314	14.363	64.354	6,972	475,070
Prisoners of War, including Service internees	180,405	9.045	26,363	8,453	14.589[2]	79,4892	8,115	326,459
Total	755,257	101,538	95.561	39,929	37.633	179.935	36,172	1,246,025

1) Including men from overseas serving in these forces, in particular from Newfoundland and Southern Rhodesia.
2) Including 20,147 officers and other ranks missing but presumed to be prisoners of war.

Colonel A. Haywood and Brigadier F.A.S. Clarke state that about 3,000 Africans 'were lost' in the 'first operation' in Burma'.[19]

There are vast differences in the numbers of colonial servicemen noted as killed: in July 1946, a total of 3,131 'West, East and Central African' deaths were reported to Parliament. Add the 220 reported to the West India Committee. But a few months previously the number of deaths for the 'Colonies' was reported as 6,877 (see above). This leaves 3,520 from un-named colonies. Where were these troops from? And historian David Killingray's recent book states that '15,000 British Africans were killed in the war'.[20] Were no accurate counts kept? Was this in order to limit the numbers of families entitled to some sort of pension?

AFRICA AND AFRICANS

By the end of the war about 450,000 East and West Africans had served in the military in Somaliland, Abyssinia (Ethiopia), East Africa and Madagascar; 120,000 served in the war against the Japanese who had invaded the British colony of Burma. Approximately 4,200 West Africans served *locally* in the **Royal Naval Voluntary Reserve** (RNVR) in each of the four colonies and others served in the RN 'Establishments' in Abyssinia, Kenya and South Africa. The RNVR had been set up mainly for patrol, escort and minesweeping duties, and also as ship repair yards. About 5,000, including 77 women, served in the **Air Services.**[21]

East Africans served in battalions of the **King's African Rifles** (KAR), which had been formed in East Africa in 1902 for both military and internal security functions. As Britain's colonies in West Africa were surrounded by 'hesitant' French colonies, Britain decided it was necessary to expand the **Royal West African Frontier Force** (RWAFF) which had originally been formed in 1900 to garrison the West African colonies. The attempt by the Royal Navy to conquer Vichy-held Dakar in 1940 failed. By the end of 1941 21 battalions had been formed to ensure safety from invasion, and then

Royal West African Frontier Force

to fight elsewhere. In 1943 they were merged into two Divisions, the 81st and 82nd. Each Division consisted of 3 brigades of 28,000 men. They were crucial to the retaking of Burma from the invading Japanese.[22]

The KAR fought against the Italians in Ethiopia and Somalia; against the Vichy French in North Africa and the Japanese in Burma. The 81st and 82nd West African Divisions of the RWAFF also fought in Ethiopia, Somalia and in the Burma campaign. There the Japanese thought they 'had an excellent physique and are very brave so fighting against these soldiers is somewhat troublesome'. Men in these two Divisions were awarded 5 DCMs, 47 Military Medals, 124 Mentions in Despatches and 17 Certificates of Gallantry.[23]

In 1942, fearful that the Vichy government would invite, or permit its Japanese allies to use Madagascar as a base, Britain decided on conquest. Brigades from South Africa, North Rhodesia, South Rhodesia and East Africa, as well as a Tanganyikan 'Field battery' invaded and retook the island. Capitulation was on 8 November 1942.

Though excluded from pointing a gun at Europeans, four West African medical units served in Italy. Formed of trained nursing orderlies from the West African Medical Corps, they took part in the landings in Sicily and Italy. Basuto labour corps were also used in Italy.[24]

About 100,000 men served in 'ancillary units' (ie, labour units – often called **'Pioneer Corps'**) in the RWAFF and the KAR. I have not been able to find full records of the numbers recruited to serve in the many labour corps. These men were paid much less than the 'combat' troops. As they 'kept the supplies coming', they were absolutely crucial in the war. They served in North Africa, the Middle East, Malta, Sicily, Lebanon, Israel and Burma.[25]

While some in the Pioneer Corps were volunteers, some, if not most, were conscripts. The means of recruiting were 'compulsion, naked and unashamed', according to the resident Commissioner in Basutoland in 1943.[26] Men for the military units were also often 'conscripted volunteers...arbitrarily sent to the army by their chiefs'. Some chiefs were paid 'recruiting expenses' by their governments. A Ghanaian chief was awarded the 'King's Medal for Chiefs' for the large numbers of recruits he had provided. Some chiefs resented conscription regulations and harboured deserters.[27]

Desertion rates were high for both Pioneers and combat troops. Apart from the low pay rates in comparison to Whites, this might have been in response to conscription and corporal punishments. Though the whipping of White soldiers had been abolished years before the war, Africans could still be whipped. After the war many ex-servicemen told researchers that 'kicking and beatings had turned them against European authority'. Those labelled as 'defaulters' were sometimes made to drill with a sandbag or large stone on their heads'.[28]

Hansard HC Debate 26 April 1944 vol 399 c772
COLONIAL TROOPS (CORPORAL PUNISHMENT)
Mr. Riley asked the Secretary of State for the Colonies whether he will look into the existing regulations prescribing corporal punishment for native troops under colonial Governments so as to remove all discrimination in the forms of punishment for the same offences as between native and British troops.
Colonel Stanley I have the whole question already under review in consultation with my right hon. Friend the Secretary of State for War.
Mr. Riley Does the right hon. and gallant Gentleman admit that at present there is discrimination in the treatment of offences as between native and British troops? Is it not the declared policy of this country that no discrimination should apply?
Colonel Stanley That Question has been addressed to and answered by my right hon. Friend the Secretary of State for War several times already.

Hansard HC Debate 24 October 1944 vol 404 cc40-1W
AFRICAN TROOPS (CORPORAL PUNISHMENT)
Mr. Sorensen asked the Secretary of State whether he can now state the result of his consideration of the need of reducing the number of offences committed by Colonial troops for which corporal punishment can be administered; and whether he is now prepared to abolish this form of punishment as is the case with white troops.
Sir J. Grigg My right hon. Friend the Secretary of State for the Colonies and I have now obtained the views of the Resident Minister in West Africa and of the East African Governors' Conference….. on the question of corporal punishment for African troops. ….. It is clear that it is not awarded capriciously… It must be borne in mind that African troops are drawn from a civil population which is subject to corporal punishment for a wider range of crimes than applies in this country. Moreover, as a result of the rapid expansion of these Forces, the maintenance of discipline in the new Armies recruited in East and West Africa presents a special problem. It is important to take no step which would impair the efficiency of our African troops at this stage of the war, and for this reason we have come to the conclusion that it would be unwise to abolish corporal punishment at this juncture.

Africans could not rise to a higher rank than Non-Commissioned Officer or the newly created rank of Warrant Officer / Platoon Commander. The RWAFF became the first regiment to break the colour-bar by sending Pvte. Seth Anthony of the Gold Coast to Sandhurst,[29] from where he graduated as a Second Lieutenant in 1942. Lt. Anthony served in Burma and by the end of the war had been promoted to the rank of Major.

In **South Africa**, there was total racial segregation and Africans were not permitted to fight against Europeans. The Cape Corps enlisted 'coloureds' (the official terminology used for 'mixed-race' people) but they could not rise in the ranks. During the war the Indian and Malay Corps and Native Military Corps were united. A total of c.92,000 men served in these Corps, doing labouring and 'technical' work – eg, driving. Though afraid of training Africans to shoot, '2,000 men from the Cape Corps were given small-arms training and deployed as garrison troops and guards in South and North Africa'. An estimated 20,000 Africans were enlisted as casual labourers on various military bases.[30]

In **Kenya** (a White settler colony[31]) in 1941 'the Colonial Secretary was very much alarmed and concerned over the reported colour bar against West African troops then stationed in Nairobi… [S]peaking on the need to wage war against colour discrimination, he emphasised that…the support of the coloured races is necessary… India and Africa…could supply millions of men and raw materials to ensure victory'.[32] A section of the all-white Kenya Regiment 'was converted into the Kenya Auxiliary Air Unit… During the East Africa campaign the [Unit] was employed in communications, reconnaissance and training tasks and for anti-submarine patrols under the Royal Navy at Mombasa.'[33]

Kenya and Uganda also served as a temporary home for about 19,000 European refugees, mainly from Poland. After the war most of them re-migrated to the UK, Canada and Australia.[34]

Freetown (Sierra Leone) became the home port of the Royal Navy's South Atlantic Command and airfields were built in **Nigeria** and the **Gold Coast** for both British and American air fleets. For example, the Africa-Middle-East Wing of the US Air Transport Command was based in Accra from early in 1942. A few months later the US based two of its Ferrying Squadrons in Accra, in anticipation of the struggle against the Japanese in Burma. Thousands of Africans were recruited for 'ground duties'. Nigeria especially became a staging post for the war in North Africa and the Middle East. It is estimated that 100,000 British and 'several thousand American troops passed through West Africa, many remaining as long as eighteen months'. This naturally required the construction of military camps, roads and much else, providing reasonably well-paid, but temporary jobs. Such vast numbers were required that in 1941 conscription was introduced in the Gold Coast for drivers and 'artisans'.[35]

West Indies and West Indians

On their newly acquired lands on the islands (see below) the **US** built **naval bases and airfields**. This was in order to protect the convoys of merchant vessels about to cross the Atlantic, which assembled in the Trinidad area. By August 1942 there were 16 German U-boats based in the Caribbean Sea, aiming to sink supply ships and bomb oil storage tanks. Just one U-boat sank nine ships in two weeks. A total of three U-boats and 192 merchant vessels were sunk. About 7,000 seamen died in Caribbean waters. U-boats penetrated the harbours of Port-of-Spain in Trinidad and Castries in St.Lucia and shelled the storage tanks on Dutch-owned Aruba in February 1942.[36]

"The Duchess of Kent at 'Warriors of the Empire' exhibition inspects portrait of Flight-Lieut P. L. U. Cross, D.SO. D.F.C".
London Gazette, 2 January 1945

As there was no recruitment for the military till 1944, some 350 West Indians enlisted by migrating to Canada. Two rose to the rank of sergeant.[37] (White West Indians had, of course, been accepted and were shipped to England.) However, as the war progressed there was such a shortage of men in the RAF, that 5,536 were recruited as ground crew and about

100 served as RAF pilots and navigators (ie, officers).[38] The most highly deco-
rated West Indian in the RAF was Ulric Cross. A Trinidadian, he was awarded
the DSO (Distinguished Service Order) and DFC (Distinguished Flying Cross
and promoted to the rank of Squadron Leader. Dudley Thompson of Jamaica
reached the rank of Flight Lieutenant in the Bomber Command.[39]

It was reported in the *Evening Standard* on 30 October 1941 that there
was a 'shortage of **Auxiliary Territorial Service** (ATS)[40] recruits…100,000
[women] were needed by
Christmas… Thousands of
pounds has been spent on
recruiting…'. As there was
no shortage of women in
the colonies, in February
1943 the CO discussed
recruiting women from
'Colonial dependencies'.
The War Office agreed
to the recruitment – but
not of 'coloured women'.

Colonel Stanley inspecting RAF recruits.
West India Committee Circular, August 1944

Eventually the disputing
government departments
agreed to recruit 30 'black
West Indians into the
British ATS'.

So a 'racially mixed
group' of one hundred
West Indian women was
enlisted. But their time
in the UK was not wholly
pleasant. According to a
report in the Jamaican
Public Opinion the 'life of

Auxiliary Territorial Service.
West India Committee Circular, August 1944

ATS girls is aggravated by petty insults and impositions… There was a slightly
veiled hostility to "these foreigners" who were making "such a beastly nuisance
of themselves".[41]

Thousands of West Indian women served in their home commands and over
1,215 men served in the local RNVR.

In February 1944 recruitment began for an army contingent for the war
front. This new **Caribbean Regiment** was formed of 1,200 volunteers, drawn
from all the British West Indies. They were sent for training to the USA and

then dispatched to North Africa and from there to Italy, where they were employed in general duties behind the front line. The Regiment never saw front line action. Richard Jacobs, who served as a 'non-commissioned officer', recalled that

Caribbean Regiment in Egypt

I travelled to the United States of America, to Italy and to Egypt where I was a victim of racial discrimination. With other members of the Regiment, I fought violent verbal and physical battles with white soldiers in the streets, hotels and night-clubs in Cairo, Suez and Alexandria.[42]

Over a thousand volunteers were recruited from all the islands for the **Trinidad Royal Naval Reserve**. The Reserve manned tugs and carried out mine-sweeping, salvage and rescue operations. There were also local defence forces. For example, the Jamaica Reserve Regiment was recruited in 1939, 'to keep order'.[43]

Deaths. According to the report in the *West India Committee Circular* (February 1946), 219 West Indians had been killed, and 265 wounded; 96 became Prisoners-of-War. But on 17 July 1946 in the House of Commons it was announced that 'no West Indian soldiers were engaged in active operations against the enemy during the war' – so none could be listed as dying. But the Committee's *Circular* notes 278 men and 32 women on 'Active Service' in the RN; 931 and 211 in the Army, and 6,050 and 77 in the RAF. So a total of 7,579. Why couldn't the British government recognise these women and men? To avoid the payment of pensions to the families of those killed?

Indians Army troops in Africa

INDIA AND INDIANS

The Indian National Congress, while simultaneously campaigning for the British to 'Quit India', did not impede recruitment to the military. About 2,500,000 Indians served in the **Indian Army** in Syria, Iraq, North Africa, East Africa, Italy, France, the Balkans, and Burma, Java and Malaya. They were crucial in the taking of Monte Cassino in Italy and with African troops bore the brunt of the fighting in Burma.[44]

The exigencies of the war meant there were simply not enough White officers to lead millions of men in the Indian army so the number of Indian officers had to be increased – and their pay was eventually raised to equal that of Whites.[45] Towards the end of the war there were almost 16,000 Indian officers.[46] From 1943 new regulations permitted Indian and British soldiers to be trained together for commissions in the Indian Army.[47]

In 1939 the **Indian Navy** had 7 small sloops; 62% of the officers were White British. By the war's end there were 35,000 seamen in the Royal Indian Navy and the officers were mainly Indians. Twenty-four Indians served in the RAF; Mahinder Singh Pujji, awarded the DFC, rose to the rank of Squadron Leader. **The Indian Air Force** was also established and by the end of the war operated nine squadrons of Spitfires and Hurricanes and had 24,000 personnel. Initially most of officers had been Whites.[48]

Parsi women in Bombay during air-raid training

Ten thousand women were recruited to the **Women's Auxiliary** and the **Women's Indian Naval Service**. About half the recruits in the Naval Service were Anglo-Indians, Christians, British women resident in India, and Burmese.[49]

India also became a **base for operations**. Two hundred airfields were built, with another seven specifically for the US air force. Massive storage buildings had to be constructed. 132,000 British (including African) and American troops had to be fed and accommodated.[50]

The many thousands of Indians guarding **Singapore** were imprisoned when the

Squadron Leader Mahinder Singh, DFC

Boy-Signallers of H.M.I.S Bahadur. (*Martial India*, 1945[48])

THE FIFTH INDIAN DIVISION'S FOUR VICTORIA CROSSES.

2ND LIEUT. (NOW MAJOR) PREMINDRA SINGH BHAGAT, ROYAL BOMBAY SAPPERS AND MINERS, RECEIVING HIS V.C. FROM FIELD-MARSHAL SIR ARCHIBALD WAVELL FOR GALLANTRY AT GONDAR, ABYSSINIA.

Major Premindra Singh Bhagat is the first King's commissioned Indian officer to gain the Victoria Cross. It was awarded in 1941. He was accompanying leading mobile troops to clear the road of mines. For four days and over a distance of fifty-five miles he led the column and supervised the clearing of fifteen minefields, often under close enemy fire. His commanding officer described his action as "one of the longest continued feats of sheer, cold courage I have ever seen."

JEM : RAM SARUP SINGH.
The V.C. was posthumously awarded to Jemadar Ram Sarup Singh, 1st Punjab Regiment, in February this year. He was in charge of a platoon which, in Burma on October 25, 1944, was ordered to put in a diversionary attack. He was twice wounded whilst leading charges and then mortally wounded.

LCE-CPL. J. P. HARMAN.
The V.C. was posthumously awarded to Lce-Cpl. Harman in June 1944 for heroic action and supreme devotion to duty on the Indo-Burma frontier on April 8, 1944. He was serving in the Queen's Own Royal West Kent Regiment, and, with great determination, charged alone with fixed bayonet and wiped out a Japanese post at Kohima.

JEMADAR ABDUL HAFIZ.
Posthumously awarded the V.C. in July 1944 for gallantry whilst attacking a Japanese position ten miles north of Imphal on April 6, Jemadar Abdul Hafiz led two sections of the 9th Jats in an attack on a strong position. He was wounded, but continued to lead his men in pursuit of the enemy and was mortally wounded.

Illustrated London News, 22 December 1945, p.682

colony was conquered by the Japanese. Some deserted and formed the Indian National Army, intent on ridding India of its British overlords.[51]

Despite not having been consulted about its entry into the war, India had to pay for its armed services, as well as for the British officers in command and the British troops stationed in India. **Defence expenditure** as a percentage of India's total annual budget during the war years rose to 81% in the peak year of 1943-4, from a 'low' of 65% in 1940-41.

Deaths. The estimate of the numbers of Indian soldiers who died varies from 24,338 to 87,000. 11,754 were reported as 'missing in action', 64,354 were wounded and 79,489 became POWs.[52] Indians won 31 Victoria Crosses and 4,000 awards for gallantry.[53]

US MILITARY IN THE COLONIES

Once America entered the war, their troops were spread around the British Empire. For example, as noted above, Accra became the headquarters of three US Ferrying Squadrons, set up for the forthcoming struggle to prevent the Japanese extending westwards from conquered Burma.

In September 1940, as Britain was in great need of naval vessels, Prime Minister Churchill signed a deal with the USA. (The US was not in the war then, but had agreed to provide various forms of support to the Allies.) Though he feared the loss of sovereignty over the islands, Churchill exchanged 99-year leases for land on the British islands for 50 American 'mothballed' destroyers. The land in Antigua, the Bahamas, British Guiana, Jamaica, St.Lucia and Trinidad, as well as Newfoundland, was to be turned into US military bases. The USA set up fourteen 'stations', varying from radio stations to airfields and naval bases.

In the opinion of Admiral of the Fleet Sir John Cunningham, 'any escort ships for our convoys...well worth their weight in gold and were certainly more use to us than a whole lot of completely undeveloped overseas bases'.[54]

The US also got involved in increasing the production of raw materials vital to the war, such as oil in Trinidad and bauxite in Jamaica. Whether US troops sent to the Caribbean should include African-Americans, was debated by the two governments. The British government feared that 'local black West Indians would become uncontrollable if black American soldiers were positioned in proximity'.[55] Was it the US policy of total segregation that the government feared, or the influence of the political struggles of African-Americans for equality?

The United States declared that it had no 'designs on the colonial possessions of other nations and no desire to carve out for its exclusive benefit any portion of Africa'. George Padmore was not convinced, arguing that 'wider markets are an absolute necessity for US capitalism, and as things stand, they can only be secured at the expense of the British Empire'.[56]

George Hall, Under-Secretary of State for the Colonies, on returning from a visit to the West Indies and Washington in October 1941 told reporters that

Britain and the United States will make a very important drive to bring about social and economic development throughout the Caribbean... Asked for his impressions of conditions in the islands, he said that in some there had been little or no progress for some time...[some[colonies were making important contributions to the war effort by the production of essential raw materials....He was also asked for assurances that on no condition would British sovereignty in the West Indies be interfered with.[57]

TUESDAY, 2 JANUARY, 1945

Air Ministry, 2nd January, 1945.

The KING has been graciously pleased to approve the following awards in recognition of gallantry displayed in flying operations against the enemy:—

Distinguished Service Order.

Acting Flight Lieutenant Philip Louis Ulric Cross, D.F.C. (133060), R.A.F.V.R., 139 Sqn.

This officer has set a fine example of keenness and devotion to duty. He has participated in a very large number of sorties, most of which have been against such heavily defended targets as Berlin, Hamburg, Ludwigshaven and industrial centres in the Ruhr area. He is a brave and resolute member of aircraft crew, whose exceptional navigational ability has been an important factor in the successes obtained. His services have been of immense value.

London Gazette, 2 January 1945

Squadron Leader Ulric Cross, DFC, DSO

NOTES

1 TNA: CO323/1672: minute by Lees, 11/9/1939.
2 TNA: INF 1/558 and 1/559: Overseas Planning Committee: Plan for propaganda to British West Africa, 1942 & 1944. See, eg, Bonny Ibhawoh, 'Second World War Propaganda, Imperial Idealism and Anti- Colonial Nationalism in British West Africa' *Nordic Journal of African Studies*, 16/2, 2007, pp.221–243; Rosaleen Smyth, 'Britain's African colonies and British propaganda during the Second World War', *Jnl. of Imperial and Commonwealth History*, 14/1, 1985, pp.65-83; Wendell P. Holbrook, 'British Propaganda and the Mobilization of the Gold Coast War Effort, 1939-1945', *Jnl. of African History*, 26/1, 1985, pp.347-361.
3 Roger Lambo, 'Achtung! The Black Prince: West Africans in the Royal Air Force, 1939 – 1946', in David Killingray (ed), *Africans in Britain*, London: Frank Cass, 1994, pp.145-163; quote is p.160.
4 Lambo (1994 –n.3), pp.155, 156.
5 Lambo (1994 –n.3), p.161.
6 The most comprehensive history is Ashley Jackson, *The British Empire and the Second World War*, New York: Hambledon Continuum 2006. See also Christopher Somerville, *Our War: How the British Commonwealth Fought the Second World War*, London: Cassell, 1998; sadly there are no references/footnotes/sources in this book.
7 Lizzie Collingham, *The Taste of War: World War Two and the Battle for Food*, London: Allen Lane, 2011, p.412.
8 Isaac Fadoyebo, *A Stroke of Unbelievable Luck*, University of Wisconsin, 1999, p.viii – edited with an introduction by David Killingray.
9 Bildad Kaggia, *Roots of Freedom*, Nairobi: East African Publishing House, 1975, p.32; Lt. Col. H.C. St.C. Whitehorne, in 'Pieces of the Past: 'Recollections of WWII', *Daily Gleaner*, www.jamaica-gleaner.com/pages/history/story/0047.htm
10 Tanzanian National Archives: TZ 32823, Army War Service Gratuities.
11 O.J.E. Shiroya, *Kenya and World War II*, Nairobi: Kenya Literature Bureau, 1985, pp.32-33; Adrienne M. Israel, 'Measuring the War Experiences: Ghanaians Soldiers in World War II', *Jnl. of African History*, 25/1, 1987, pp.161.
12 Tanzanian National Archives: TZ 32856, Army War Service Gratuities – Africans.
13 David Smith, 'They fought for Britain. In return they were given £10', *Observer*, 3/9/2006. The article is based on an interview with the son of Richard Chandaengerwa, who served for three years in the Rhodesian African Rifles.
14 D.H. Barber, *Africans in Khaki*, London: Edinburgh House Press, 1948, p.54.
15 Timothy H. Parsons, *The African Rank-and-File*, NH: Heinemann, 1999, p.237; David Killingray with Martin Plaut, *Fighting for Britain: African Soldiers in the Second World War*, Woodbridge: James Currey, 2010, pp.191-2, 197-199.
16 *West Africa*, 1/12/1945; 27/10/1945.
17 *West Africa*, 27/10/1945. See www.nationalarchives.gov.uk/documentsonline/wo373.asp. For lists of awards to Indian military (mostly awarded to the British

officers), see, http://www.hut-six.co.uk/WW2data/WO373-82.html and //www. hut-six.co.uk/WW2data/WO373-Burma%20and%20India.html. For awards in the Burma campaign, see www.chindits.info/Awards/Awards%20List.html.

18 David Killingray, 'African voices from two world wars', *Historical Research*, 74/186, November 2001, pp.425-443; Somerville (1998 – n.6), pp.191-193; Norman Clothier, 'The Erinpura: Basotho Tragedy', *Military History Journal*, 8/5, 1991, available on http://samilitaryhistory.org/vol085nc.htmlhttp://en.wikipedia.org/ wiki/SS_Khedive_Ismail.

19 Col. A. Haywood & Brigadier F.A.S. Clarke, *History of the RWAFF*, Aldershot: Gale & Polden, 1964, p.411. The *West African Review* reported in its January 1946 issue that in the Burma campaign 998 West Africans had been killed, 185 were 'missing' and 3,055 had been wounded. (p.13)
For an interesting assessment of the future of the RWAFF, see Major M.N. Hennessy, 'The Royal West African Frontier Force Looks Ahead', *African World*, December 1948, pp.13-15.

20 *Hansard*, 17/7/1946, vol.425, cc.217-21W; Killingray (2010 – n.15), p.8 (no source is given for the numbers); *West India Committee Circular*, February 1946. It must be noted that the Committee only had data for those who had *registered* with it.

21 Data from *West African Review*, March 1946, p.308. See E.E. Sabben-Clare, 'African Troops in Asia', *African Affairs*, 44/177, October 1945, pp.155-157; Lord Swinton, 'West Africa's Contribution to the War', *Colonial Review*, December 1943, p.108; Sir William Platt, 'Lessons of the East Africa Command', *Colonial Review*, March 1946, pp.148-149; R.H. Kankembo, *An African Soldier Speaks*, London: Livingstone Press, 1947; David Killingray, 'Military and labour recruitment in the Gold Coast during the Second World War', *Journal of African History*, #23, 1982, p.83 and Killingray, (2001 – n.18). Data on the naval 'Establishments' is from correspondence with the Ministry of Defence in August/September 1994. It was then pointed out to me that the numbers serving were not available, as 'the majority' only served as 'locally engaged personnel'. An excellent source of information is Sir John Shuckburgh, *Colonial Civil History of the War* (Colonial Office, c.1949, but not published). He produced the book for the Cabinet Office in his capacity as the official historian of the colonial empire in the war. Shuckburgh had been Deputy Under-Secretary at the Colonial Office, then-governor of Nigeria 1940-1942, when he was recalled to work in the Cabinet Office on this history. A copy is available at London University's Senate House Library.

22 *West Africa*, October 1948, p.1121. See 'Coloured Soldiers in Italy', *Picture Post*, 29 July 1944.

23 Killingray (2001 – n.18), p.437. There were reports of the African troops in Burma by George Padmore in the *Chicago Defender*. See, eg., issues for 27/2/1944 & 21/7/1944. Report of medals is in *West Africa*, 1/12/1945.

24 *RWAFF News*, #121, 4/9/1944.

25 Ministry of Defence, *We Were There* (nd), pp.26, 42; Peter B. Clarke, *West Africans at War*, London: Ethnographica 1986, p.20; Jackson (2006 – n.6),

p.182. Timothy H. Parsons states that by March 1941 38,084 Kenyans had been recruited, but almost 92% served in the labour forces. (*The African Rank-and-File*, NH: Heinemann, 1999. p.73) For many brief biographies, see Erica Myers-Davis, *Under One Flag*, London: Get Publishing, 2009; and Chapter 3 in Warahiu Itote, *'Mau Mau' General*, Nairobi: East Africa Publishing House, 1967. On the KAR, see also John Nunneley, *Tales from the King's African Rifles*, London: Cassell, 1998. (He was a British recruit sent to serve in the KAR in 1942.)

26 Quoted in D. Killingray, 'Labour exploitation for military campaigns in British Colonial Africa', *Jnl. of Contemporary History*, 24/3, 1989, p.483.

27 Killingray (1982 –n.21), p.89. D.H. Barber, who served as an officer in one of the East African Pioneer Corps, reported that when he asked a senior officer if the Africans were conscripted, he was told that 'It varies in different parts of Africa. In some parts each tribal chief is asked to provide a certain number of recruits. If he can obtain as many volunteers as he wants he will no doubt accept them; otherwise he will conscript. In other parts of Africa, for instance Basutoland, volunteers have come forward in large numbers.' D.H. Barber, *Africans in Khaki*, London: Edinburgh Press, 1948, p.3; on p.9 he states that 'recruits were conscripts'.

28 David Killingray, 'The "Rod of Empire": The Debate over Corporal Punishment in the British African Colonial Forces, 1888-1946', *Jnl. of African History*, 35/2, 1994, p.211. The data suggests that African were more likely to be beaten in the KAR than the RWAFF. (p.213); Adrienne M. Israel, 'Measuring the War Experience', *Jnl. of Modern African Studies*, 25/1, 1987, p.163.

29 Sandhurst was – and is – the Royal Military Academy where all officers in the British Army are trained. On Seth Anthony, see eg obituary on http://www.modernghana.com/news/198470/1/obituary-major-seth-anthony. html by Cameron Duodu.

30 Jackson (2006 - n.6), p.242.

31 In 1939 the population of Kenya was 1.8 million Africans, 55,710 'Asiatics' and almost 15,000 Europeans. (Kenya *Blue Book*, 31/12/1938 – this is the annual statistical report from the colonial governments.) The accuracy of the data on Africans must be questioned.

32 G.O. Olusanya, 'The Role of Ex-Servicemen in Nigerian Politics', *Jnl. of Modern African Studies*, 6/2, 1968, p.223.

33 Jackson (2006 –n.6), p.383.

34 Curtis Abraham, 'When Europeans were refugees in Africa', *New African Magazine*, June 2012, pp.72-77.

35 Killingray (1982 – n.21), pp.86, 89; James S. Coleman, *Nigeria: Background to Nationalism*, Benin City: Broburg & Wistrom, 1986, p.25; Shiroya (1985 – n.11), p.3.

36 Humphrey Metzgen & John Graham, *Caribbean Wars Untold*, University of West Indies Press, 2007. p.194, pp.223-4; Ken Post, *Strike The Iron: A Colony at War: Jamaica 1939-1945*, Atlantic Highlands: Humanities Press, 1981, p.245; Michael Anthony, *Port-of-Spain in a World at War 1939-1945*, Port-of-Spain,

Trinidad: Paria Publishing (1978), 2008, volume 2, p.120.

37 Owen Rowe, 'Reflections of a World War Two Veteran', *Akili Newsletter* 1/3, November 1993. According to this article it was campaigning by the Canada West India League that forced the Canadian military to accept Blacks.

38 See Edward Scobie, 'Caribbean Wings', *Flamingo*, August 1952. And these memoirs: Eric Ferron, *"Man, You've Mixed": a Jamaican Comes to Britain*, London: Whiting & Birch, 1995; Amos A. Ford, *Telling the Truth: The life and Times of the British Honduran Forestry Unit in Scotland, 1941-4*, London: Karia Press, 1985; Cy Grant, *"A Member of the RAF of Indeterminate Race": WW2 experiences of a former RAF Navigator & POW*, Bognor Regis: Woodfield, 2006; Sam King, *Climbing Up the Rough Side of the Mountain*, London: Minerva Press, 1998; Robert N. Murray, *Lest We Forget: The Experiences of World War II Westindian Ex-Service Personnel*, Nottingham Westindian Ex-Services Association, 1996; E. Martin Noble, *Jamaica Airman*, London: New Beacon Books, 1984. There is now a useful website http://www.caribbeanaircrew-ww2.com/?p=6.

39 See Dudley Thompson, *From Kingston to Kenya: The Making of a Pan-Africanist Lawyer*, Dover, Mass.: The Majority Press, 1993. There is a brief history of Ulric Cross and some other 'contributors' in Stephen Bourne, *The Motherland Calls*: Stroud: The History Press, 2012.

40 Initially the women in the ATS did labouring work as cleaners, cooks, drivers, postal workers. As the war progressed, they began to 'man' anti-aircraft guns and became orderlies, ammunition inspectors and also worked at jobs previously only held by men such as welders, carpenters, electricians, drivers, motor mechanics, etc.

41 Ben Bousquet & Colin Douglas, *West Indian Women at War: British Racism in World War II*, London: Lawrence & Wishart, 1991, pp.102, 107, 151-153; *Public Opinion* 12/3/1945, p.1. Among the recollections of war veterans published in the Barbados paper, *The Nation*, in November-December 1982, are those of Odessa Gittens who served in the ATS.

42 George Weekes, 'Butler and the OWTU', in W. Richard Jacobs (ed), *Butler Versus The King: riots and sedition in 1937*, Port-of-Spain: Key Caribbean Publications, 1976, p.154.

43 Post (1981 – n.36) p.58; Shuckburgh (nd – n.21), p.62. I asked the Ministry of Defence for the numbers serving in the RNVRs, but they could not tell me. (correspondence August & September 1994)

44 There are many books on the Indian armies. See, eg, Philip Mason, *A Matter of Honour*, London: Macmillan, 1974. On the war in North Africa, see *The Tiger Kills: the story of the Indian Divisions in the North African Campaign*, 'published by His Majesty's Stationery Office for the Government of India', 1944.

45 Ministry of Defence, *We Were There* (nd), pp.32, 36, 38; Byron Farwell, *Armies of the Raj: From Mutiny to Independence, 1858-1947*, London: Viking, 1989, chapter 20, 'Indianization'; Lawrence James, *Raj: The Making and Unmaking of British India*, New York: St.Martin's Press, 1997, pp.545, 589.

46 V.G. Kiernan, *Colonial Empires and Armies 1815 – 1960*, Stroud: Sutton Publishing, 1998, p.205.

47 *Chicago Defender*, 9/1/1943, p.1.
48 F. Yeats-Brown, *Martial India*, London: Eyre & Spottiswoode, 1945, pp.74, 114, 123; Air Marshal M.S. Chaturvedi, *History of the Indian Air Force*, New Delhi: Vikas Publishing, 1978.
49 Yeats-Brown (1945 – n.48) p.140.
50 Pradeep Barua, 'Imperial Defence: Britain and India, 1919-1956', *Jnl. of Imperial and Commonwealth History*, 25/2, 1997, pp.240-266 (data from p.260)
51 See the very interesting A.J. Bevan, *The story of Zarak Khan*, London: Arrow Books, 1956; republished 1965.
52 Barua (1997 – n.50) , p.259; Farwell (1989 – n.45), p,316. The numbers given in the House of Commons on 10/4/1945 are 19,420 killed, 13,327 missing; 51,038 wounded; POWs, 79,701 (including 21,181 'officers and other ranks missing but presumed to be prisoners of war'.
53 Farwell (1989 – n.45), p.314. For some memoirs by ex-servicemen living in Slough, England, see Un-divided Indian Ex-servicemen's Association/ English Heritage, *Remembering Forgotten Heroes*, the booklet accompanying an exhibition which toured England in 2005.
54 Philip Goodhart, *Fifty Ships that Saved the World*, London: Heinemann, 1965, p.237.
55 M.M. Morehouse, 'Military service, governance and the African Diaspora', *African and Black Diaspora*, 4/1, 2011, p.51.
56 Henry Villard (Dept. of State) quoted in *New York Times*, 20/8/1943; GP: 'Blue-Print of Post-War Anglo-American Imperialism', *Left*, October 1943, p.198.
57 *Times*, 6/10/1941, p.4.

[How difficult it is to discover who was paid a pension is indicated in my recent correspondence with the Royal Commonwealth Ex-Services League. Capt. Gill explained that 'the ex-servicemen qualify for a war disability pension as a result of war service during World War II, 1939-45; the pension would have been awarded by a British Medical Board and would equate to the level of disability…. If a soldier or widow (of a serviceman killed on active service) did qualify for a pension the responsibility for paying that pension was transferred on independence to the Government of that country, but whether this actually materialised is questionable.' To me, whether there were sufficient Medical Boards is as 'questionable' as the actual payments. (Correspondence December 2012 – January 2013. with Captain Lance Gill, Controller Welfare, Royal Commonwealth Ex-Services League.) The National Army Museum appears to have no data and could not tell me if there was a difference between wages/conditions for 'regular' troops and labour corps. (Correspondence with Robert Fleming, Information & Community Outreach Curator, National Army Museum Dec. 2012 – January 2013)]

CHAPTER 4

Other Contributions by the Colonies

Financial

Perhaps not surprisingly, there is insufficient data available on this very important issue. Hence what is below I feel sure is only a partial account of such contributions.

India, as noted previously, was forced to spend over 80% of its income on the war. It had to pay for the British Army in India as well as for the Indian troops. India also had to pay the salaries and pensions of all British civil servants working in India. After the conquest of Singapore in January 1942, about half a million Allied troops were marshalled in India to prepare for the fight against the Japanese conquerors. India had not only to feed the troops but also had to provide accommodation, clothing and services.[1]

The Nawab of Bhopal bought a whole squadron of Spitfires for the RAF, and the Nizam of Hyderabad donated £170,000 for a corvette for the Royal Indian Navy. The Maharajah of Gwalior 'raised and trained seven thousand men'. Other wealthy men also made large donations and by mid-1943 'over £6.5 million had been contributed to the Viceroy's War Purposes fund'. One and a half million pounds was raised by 'ordinary' people for the Red Cross.[2]

By the war's end, the UK owed India £1.3 billion for manufactures, etc.[3]

The impoverished **Caribbean** governments also had to contribute: for example, of Trinidad's total revenue of £30.6 million for the period 1940-1945, 6.3% went on war loans and 12.0% on 'military and naval service'. By March 1943 the half million people of Trinidad had contributed over half a million pounds to various war funds and three and a half million dollars to War Loans. They bought their third bomber for the RAF in July 1942.[4] This was at a time when, for example, a male agricultural labourer was paid a maximum of two shillings per day, and a woman one and a half shillings.[5] Other contributions were more specific: for example, the one and a quarter million Jamaicans raised the funds to build 8 warplanes[6] and for a mobile canteen.

West Africans donated well over £1.5 million for various war-time funds. Nigeria's Emir of Katsina and the Emir of Daura donated the cost of a tank.

Some of the Chiefs receiving monthly salaries donated a fixed amount per month.[7] *The Times* noted on 17 January 1941 (p.3) that 'well over £50,000 has been voluntarily contributed by all races, communities and classes of the population of the Territory of Tanganyika'.[8]

Hansard HC Deb 21 October 1943 vol 392 c1528	
COLONIAL EMPIRE (WAR CONTRIBUTION)	
Mr. Creech Jones asked the Secretary of State for the Colonies the total money gifts, loans and other grants and contributions by the Colonial Empire to the war effort by Britain?	
Mr. Emrys-Evans Apart from the contributions of some Colonial Governments towards the cost of their local military forces, the total contribution of the Colonial Empire towards the prosecution of the war now amounts in round figures to £48,000,000 made up as follows:	
Gifts	£ 23,300,000.00
Loans free of interest	£ 10,700,000.00
Interest bearing loans	£ 14,000,000.00

Historians Metzger and Graham point out that financial contributions were just part of the donations from the mainly impoverished peoples of the colonies, who also raised the money to purchase mobile canteens, recreation huts and even aircraft. The total 'Gifts' from the Colonies had increased to just over £24 million by the end of the war.[9]

RAW MATERIALS

From the **Caribbean** came two absolute essentials, oil and over 2 million tons of bauxite to be made into aluminium. Oil from Trinidad was a crucial resource as it provided fuel for the RAF and was shipped, for example, to the battles in North Africa. The islands also sent timber and cotton; foods such as cocoa, coffee, rum, rice and bananas, as well as tobacco. The export of non-essentials was reduced due to the danger to ships crossing the Atlantic.

Africa became a major source of food: for example, 132,000 heads of cattle were sent to Britain from Tanganyika. The White farmers settled in East Africa demanded high prices for their food products, often produced by very low-paid conscripted labour. African farmers were always paid much less for the same products. East Africans supplied much of the food for the military in Greece, Egypt, the Balkans, Syria and Iraq.[10]

Palm oil for tin-plating and ground nuts for margarine came from Gambia. Wood, palm oil, groundnuts, coal, cocoa, columbite and tin came in large quantities from Nigeria. Industrial diamonds and iron ore came from Sierra Leone and pyrethrum (for insecticides and fertilizers) from East Africa. Other exports in vast quantities were sodium (177,000 tons from Kenya) and manganese, tin, copper (mainly from Northern Rhodesia, now Zambia), rubber (from Nigeria) and sisal, all required for the manufacture of weaponry. Bauxite, diamonds, manganese and rubber were supplied by the Gold Coast. Much tobacco came from Southern Rhodesia (now Zimbabwe). In 1941 the Belgian government-in-exile put the resources of its colony, Congo, in the hands of the British government. Now the Allies had access to more copper, and to diamonds, radium and cobalt. The uranium needed for the development of the atomic bomb also came from the Congo.[11]

Nigerian cocoa earned £2.7 million in much needed US dollars.[12]

SELECTED EXPORTS: COLONIES AND INDIA, 1939-45				
COUNTRY	**PRODUCT**	**1939**	**1942**	**1945**
Tanganyika	Cattle – heads	9,006	65,806	56,944
	Diamonds - carats	3,445	40,237	115,620
Kenya	Wheat – tons	3,150	3,500	5,950
	Pyrethrum – tons	2,800	5.250	5,400
	Tea – lbs	9,925	11,488	9,477
	Sodium - tons	40,585	64,537	72,182
Gold Coast	Rubber – tons	678	1,862	1,570
(Ghana)	Bauxite - tons	0	48	146
Nigeria	Rubber – tons	2,824	6,667	10,517
	Tin - tons	14,554	16,557	15,166
Barbados	Rum – thou. gls.	82	488	1,088
Trinidad	Spirits – gls	9,426	30,603	49,564
	Oil – mill. gls.	359	?	118
Br. Guinea	Bauxite – tons	476,000	1,116,000	739,000
(Guyana)	Gum - tons	244	340	289
		1939-40	**1942-43**	**1944-45**
India	Fish – tons	17,200	17,800	20,250
	Grain/pulses – tons	73,700	38,880	25,500
	Sugar	16,750	30,750	6,650
	Manganese – tons	719,000	577,000	157,000
	Cloth – mill. yds.	221	819	423

NB Data is for exports only. As the war progressed an increasing proportion of produce was used locally for war purposes, e.g. to feed, clothe and house troops. Data mainly from *Statistical Abstracts of the British Commonwealth*, London 1947.

Much of the production was by **'conscripted' workers**. For example, Southern Rhodesia passed a Compulsory Native Labour Act in 1942 and Kenya passed a similar Act in 1943. The workers were 'recruited' by the governments for private, profit-making companies, and worked for a pittance.

To give just one example, according to Anarchist's (name used by author) article in *War Commentary* (Mid-April, 1942) there were 20,000 forced labourers, aged 16+, working for a minimum of 84 days annually on White-owned farms in Kenya.[13]

That these conscripts were working for companies which were making vast profits, was eventually raised in Parliament. *The Times* reported on 27 November 1943 that 'the whole question of the use of conscript labour in private undertakings throughout the colonial dependencies was receiving the attention of his Majesty's Government, and that no further extensions should be made pending their decision'. But the use of conscripts was not suspended.

Conditions were so bad that complaints occasionally even reached the Colonial Office (CO). For example, in the tin mines in Nigeria (privately owned by British companies) the CO found that diet and clothing were inadequate, overcrowding was gross, and meningitis, diarrhoea and dysentery were widespread. Men were supposedly conscripted for 16 weeks, three times a year, so some could have had to work in these mines almost for a full year. Desertion was common. In a telegram to the Nigerian Governor the CO advised that compulsory labour should be stopped from the end of April 1944.[14]

Despite much censorship in Britain, on 7 December 1940 the *New Statesman* printed information on an attempted strike some months previously for higher wages by Africans working in copper mines in Rhodesia. Though White workers had been permitted to strike in 1939, now a strike by Africans was forbidden. The government ordered the military to disband the strikers; 17 were killed and 70 were injured. The mines had just announced a profit of £6 million. Africans' wages were from 9 to fourteen pence per day.[15]

While wages varied, the maximum pay in much of Africa was one shilling (twelve pence) a day. It is unclear whether all conscripted labourers were in fact paid,

India produced jute, tea, grain, fruits, fish, oils, tobacco, meat and about 1,453,000 tons of manganese for the British war effort. It also produced all the food for the Indian military and the British troops stationed there.

MANUFACTURES

Manufacturing was not permitted in the colonies. India had a somewhat different status, so an estimated five million Indians worked in war industries. Indian workers produced 17 million uniforms, 5 million blankets, 372,000 leather jackets 16 million pairs of boots and 5 million pairs of shoes as well as many thousands of tents to accommodate soldiers. India produced the silk for man-dropping parachutes, and by 1944 manufactured 200,000 supply-dropping cotton parachutes per month. Medicines were also produced. New steel mills were built and manufactured, for example, the body parts for vehicles for which engines and chassis were imported. Ordinance factories were then also built.[16]

Merchant Navy

When the war broke out, 'coloured' seamen received not only lower wages, but also a lower 'war bonus' than Whites. They were often employed on ships with the worst living conditions.[17] The first strike on this issue was in October 1939 and there were many more, in Cardiff, Liverpool, Glasgow.[18] In 1942 Lascar (Indian seamen) wages (including the war bonus) were increased to £6.75 while British Whites received £24.00 per week for the same work.

It was not till the end of the war that the seamen's struggle was over. At long last the National Maritime Board and the National Union of Seamen agreed that Black and White crew were to be paid the same wages and work under the same conditions.

It is estimated that by 1944 there were 145,000 merchant seamen, of whom c.29,000 were Lascars and perhaps 21,750 were 'colonials'. Death numbers are also estimated: about 30,000 merchant seamen died, of whom at least 5,000 were 'colonials'. There was a high death rate for colonial seamen as most 'were employed in the engine room of old coal burning ships and those were the last to scramble to safety'.[19]

That a WWII West Indian merchant seaman had not been paid his pension was reported by *The Voice*, on 9 April 1996. The Ministry of Defense promised to investigate. Had others received their pensions? (Whether pensions had been paid to the widows of the Lascar seamen was questioned at the 1996 meeting of the International Transport Federation in London.)

Colonial Workers in Britain

Despite whipping up much propaganda for the need to support the Mother Country, the colonial governments were told in 1939 and again in 1940 that 'it is not desired that non-Europeans British subjects should come here for enlistment'.[20] This referred to colonials volunteering to go to the UK to work in various industries. However, as the labour shortage increased vastly as the war went on and on, the British government considered importing West Indian agricultural workers, but then decided that 'from the employers' point of view they would be found unsatisfactory'.[21] Eventually it was decided, perhaps to avoid bad publicity, to import a token number of skilled workers and 'industrial trainees'. About 345 West Indians were recruited in 1941-2 and dispersed to various, mainly munitions, factories in the North-East. The warden of West

Indies House, a segregated hostel for some of the men, reported on the racism often confronted by the workers.[22]

Most of the men were housed in hostels – some of these accepted all workers, (eg the YMCA hostels) others were segregated. The men's experience was mixed: there is some evidence of acceptance by fellow workers, but more of racial discrimination, including that of trade unions. The scheme was abandoned in 1943 'owing to the shortage of shipping and other difficulties', according to a CO official. Most of the men remained employed till the end of the war when they were offered repatriation. 102 accepted this, only to confront 'acute unemployment' when they reached home.[23]

YMCA hostels

In 1941 750 British Hondurans (Belize) 'foresters' were imported to work in Scotland. This might have been in response to the Governor advising the Colonial Office in 1939 that 'suffering and uneasiness acute in Belize. Due to unemployment. Developing into a dangerous situation.' But there was no help from Britain. A year later the Labour Officer informed the CO that 'our immediate problem is unemployment with attendant starvation and social unrest'.[24] Though the Ministry of Supply was reluctant, it was decided to recruit experienced 'foresters' to work in Scotland. The first contingent arrived in the winter of 1941 and the second in the winter of 1942 - not the best time to arrive in Scotland from the tropics.

The men were given inadequate clothing, housing and medical care. Their logging experience had been with totally different trees/timber, so they were deemed unskilled and paid the lowest wage. Relations with local people and with the various government departments was so problematic that, despite the labour shortage in Britain, most were repatriated in 1943. Some remained and managed to find other work. A few attempted to enlist, but were refused. 'The admiralty felt that colonial coloured volunteers were rather an embarrassment and difficult to place in this country...it was the same story with the RAF', noted the CO Welfare Officers trying to help the men.[25]

Forestry workers in Scotland

West Indian Workers in the USA

As wages there were much higher than on the islands, by 1944 there were an estimated 24,000 West Indians, mainly Jamaicans, working in the USA helping the war effort.

BRITAIN SAYS THANKS

Towards the end of the war, the Secretary of State for the Colonies admitted in Parliament that most of the funds allocated to the colonies under the 1940 Colonial Welfare and Development Act had not in fact been used. More would be done in the future, he assured the questioning MPs. And Oliver Stanley even admitted that 'I do not believe any of us would be here today … if it had not been for the Colonial Empire. It is not only their contribution in manpower and material resources. If we had not had our convoy assembling point at Freetown or our Trans-African reinforcement routes for the Middle East, I do believe this country would not have survived during the period when we had to stand alone.'

So, naturally, the Empire had to be retained and somehow merged, especially from the perspective of the new world being forged: 'the amalgamation of this country and the Colonial Empire…can really contribute power and support to world organisation, far greater in its utility than the contribution that could be made by the United Kingdom alone, and 35 separate Colonial territories', argued the Secretary of State for the Colonies.[26]

—   —   —

NOTES

1   Madhusree Mukerjee, *Churchill's Secret War*, New York: Basic Books, 2010, p.62. Pradeep Barua notes that 'The total value of the supplies given to the US forces in India totalled £129,180,000'. ('Imperial Defence: Britain and India 1919-1945', *Jnl. of Imperial and Commonwealth History*, 25/2, 1997, p.260.) For historic details of the payments India had to make to Britain for its military, which was used 'not so much for the defence of India as for the preservation and expansion of the British Empire', see S.N. Agarwala, *Indian Public Finance: Defence Expenditure in India*, Bombay: Vora Publishers, 1967; quotes are from pp.90, 93.

2   Ashley Jackson, *The British Empire and the Second World War*, New York: Hambledon Continuum 2006, p.360; Byron Farwell, *Armies of the Raj*, London: Viking, 1989, p.312; F. Yeats-Brown, *Martial India*, London: Eyre & Spottiswoode, 1945, pp.132, 154.

3   Jackson (2006 - n.2), p.356; Barua (1997 – n.1), p.260.

4   See reports in the *Crown Colonist* from October 1940 and Jackson (2006 – n.2), pp.81, 83, 84, 138, 202.

5   There were twenty shillings in a pound, so today we would call two shillings ten pence.

6   *LCP Newsletter*, November 1940, pp.32-3

7   E.I. Ekpenyon, *Some Experiences of an African Air-Raid Warden*, London: Sheldon Press, c.1945, p.14.

8   Tanganyika had been ceded to Britain by Germany, its previous colonial master, after WWI. According to the 1931 census, the African population was 5 million; there were 38,398 'Asiatics' and 8,228 Europeans. Census data on Africans has to be viewed with circumspection. 'Asiatics' were mainly Indians imported as labourers, as well as some Arabs, as there was much trade with the Arabian peninsula.

9   Humphrey Metzgen & John Graham, *Caribbean Wars Untold*, University of West Indies Press, 2007, p.194, pp.115-118; *Empire*, 21/10/1943.

10 Jackson (2006 - n.2) pp.175-6; D. Anderson & D. Throup, 'Africans and Agricultural Production in Colonial Kenya', *Jnl. of African History*, 26/4, 1985, pp.327-345; Lizzie Collingham, *The Taste of War: World War Two and the Battle for Food*, London: Allen Lane, 2011, pp. 132, 135.

11 Jackson (2006 – n.2), pp.85, 177, 179, 216, 223, 225, 226.

12 Collingham (2011 – n.10) p.140; Raymond Dumett, 'Africa's Strategic Minerals During the Second World War', *Jnl. of African History*, 26/4, 1985, pp.381-408.

13 See eg, David Killingray, 'Labour Exploitation for Military Campaigns in British Colonial Africa 1870-1945', *Jnl. of Contemporary History*, 24/3, 1989, pp.483-501. In Kenya, Whites had 'acquired' 88% of the arable land.

14 TNA: CO583/263 (30569), Secretary of State for the Colonies to Officer Administrating Government of Nigeria, 3/1/1944.

15 This is also reported in *Empire*, May 1940.

16 Mukerjee (2010 – n.1), p.222; Farwell (1989 - n.2) p.308.

17 An example of conditions was reported in the *New Leader* on 2/5/1942: there had been a riot by Chinese sailors, who claimed their 'wages were the lowest among Allied seamen…compensation for death and injury less… boarding houses rotten…20 in a room with no bathrooms…have to wash in buckets'.

18 'British Tars Win Bonus', *New Journal & Guide*, 28/10/1939, p.3; Marika Sherwood,'Race, Nationality and Employment among Lascar Seamen 1660 to 1945', *New Community*, January 1991, p.241. See also, eg., Tony Lane, *The Merchant Seamen's War*, Manchester University Press, 1990, chapter on 'Sons of Empire'.

19 Sir John Shuckburgh, *Colonial Civil History of the War*, Colonial Office, unpublished, ref. DC11806, p.63. The total number of merchant seamen who died during WWII seems unclear. According to Arthur Marsh & Victoria Ryan, it was c. 32,000. (*The Seamen*, Malthouse Press, 1989, p.149); R. Hope states that 50,525 died. (*A New History of British Shipping*, London; John Murray, 1990, p.383); 'Colonial' seamen included Chinese. The total death numbers given in Parliament on 29 November 1945 were 30,189; 'missing', 5,264; wounded, 4,402. No numbers were given for lascar/colonial deaths.

20 TNA: CAB 68/4, CO to Cabinet, 6/1/1940, quoted in Marika Sherwood. *Many Struggles: West Indian Workers and Service Personnel in Britain, 1939-1945*, London: Karia Press, 1985, p.53. See also Gavin Schaffer, 'Fighting Racism: Black Soldiers and Workers in Britain during the Second World War', *Immigrants & Minorities*, 28/2-3, July/November 2010, pp.246-265.

21 TNA: LAB13/37.

22 Alex Watkinson, 'West Indian Volunteer Technicians', *Time & Tide*, 11/7/1942.

23 Some stayed to take up offers of free education. For a full account of their recruitment, work experience etc, see Sherwood (1985 - n.20), chapter 2; quotes are from pp.83, 88. See also Anthony Richmond, *Colour Prejudice in Britain*, London: Routledge & Kegan Paul, 1954, and Carlton Wilson, '"In Their Own Words": West Indian Technicians in Liverpool During World War II', *Jnl. of Caribbean Studies*, 8/1-2, 1990-1991.

24 Sherwood (1985 – n.20), pp.71-87, 101.

25 Sherwood (1985 – n.20), p.121. Chapter 3 in this book is on the Hondurans. See also Amos Ford's account in his *Telling the Truth: The Life and Times of the British Honduran Forestry Unit in Scotland (1941-44)* London: Karia Press, 1985.

26 *Hansard*, 7/2/1945, vol. 407, cols. 2092 ff.

SECTION 3

THE 'HOME FRONTS'

It is seldom acknowledged that there could have been a 'home front' in the colonies. While admittedly they were not bombed by the Luftwaffe, fighting against the Axis was often 'next door' – for example in East Africa and India. This meant not only that many were recruited to serve in the military, but that civilians had to cope with the influx of many thousands of soldiers and with the possibility of invasion.

As noted in Chapter 4, many in the colonies worked for the war, in the fields, mines and factories. Some of these workers were 'conscripted'. Except when they were building bases for the Americans, wages were very low and could not keep pace with the rise in the cost of food. And there were often food shortages. There were hurricanes and famines.

Protest marches, trade unions and all political activities were forbidden; thousands were imprisoned, and in India gunned down. Censorship was even heavier than in Britain. Examples of what the 'home front' meant in the colonies are in Chapter 5.

While many books have been written about the 'home front' in Britain, these almost never look at the fairly ubiquitous racial discrimination both in civilian and military life. Nor do we acknowledge the services rendered by the Black population. Just to give one example: Dr. Bhandari 'offers medical service' to the people in the shelters during bombing raids on East London, according to Frank Lewey, the Mayor of Stepney in his very interesting book, *Cockney Campaign* (1944). He 'treats four hundred nightly...' (p.109).

Chapter 6 focuses on racial discrimination and gives some examples of the political activities of the Black and Indian organisations in Britain.

Mohandas Gandhi released from prison in 1944

CHAPTER 5

THE 'HOME FRONT' IN THE COLONIES

INDIA

In June 1940 the British government passed the **India and Burma Emergency Bill**, which 'introduced compulsory service for the military, and in certain cases for civil industrial purposes'.[1] Noting the 'curtain of censorship', the *New Statesman* on 14 December 1940 (p.611) reported that 'The Defence of India Act was used to round up everyone whom the Anglo-Indian police viewed with suspicion or disapproval'. Eighteen members of provincial governments as well as Jawaharlal Nehru were now in jail.[2]

To attempt to overcome the resistance of the Indian National Congress to participate in the war, Britain sent out Sir Stafford Cripps[3] with an offer of dominion status after the war's end, and the secession of provinces with a Muslim majority. It was rejected by the Congress Party and the Muslim League. After some discussion a movement of civil disobedience, demanding immediate independence was begun. On 8 August 1942 the **'Quit India' movement** was announced by the All-India Congress Committee, led by Mohandas Gandhi and Jawaharlal Nehru. It was a war cry for Indians: 'The presence of the British in India is an invitation to Japan to invade India. Their withdrawal removes that bait...', said Gandhi. In London, Prime Minister Winston Churchill reported to the House of Commons on September 10 that 'only 500' Indians had been killed putting down the civil disobedience. Some had been killed by the Indian police, some by the British military.[4]

Now (ie, after the Quit India announcement) Gandhi, Nehru and most other leaders and political figures were arrested. 'The Congress was outlawed for three years...its funds were seized and its organisation virtually broken.'[5] This led to much violence on the streets, and further arrests. The Government issued an order banning public processions, meetings and assemblies. In the ensuing protests, 1,028 were killed, including by machine guns fired from low-flying aircraft, and 3,200 wounded. According to Nehru, during the war **the total numbers imprisoned** were between 25,000 and 30,000; a further 10,000 were shot 1943-5.[6] The CID infiltrated Congress, to obtain information on all forthcoming protests. Nevertheless, they continued, as did shootings and imprisonments. Almost nothing was known of these murders in Britain, due to the war-time censorship.[7]

While many were already going hungry due to the increase in prices, in October 1943 there was a massive **famine** in Bengal and Orissa, caused mainly by a cyclone: thousands of square miles of crop-bearing land were damaged. The situation was exacerbated by the conquest of Burma by Japan, as Bengal had traditionally imported rice from there. Nevertheless, India exported small quantities of food to meet the needs of the British-Indian and the Ceylon Armies abroad. The Indian government ignored the famine, as did Winston Churchill in England – it was not till the end of 1944 that some food relief was sent by England. The estimates of the death count vary between 2 and 4 million. Major Yeats-Brown reported that about '12 million people in Bengal were suffering from the effects of famine'.[8]

Naturally the **Atlantic Charter**, which promised self-government (see Chapter 7) was welcomed by Indians. When Churchill maintained that it was inapplicable to India, the whole country was infuriated. One Indian member of the Viceroy's Legislative Council remarked that 'Indians were dying to emancipate others while their countrymen remained enslaved'. The President of the Hindu Mahasabha (the Hindu Nationalist Party) appealed directly to President Roosevelt, and asked him whether America would guarantee India's post-war freedom'.[9]

Mahatma Gandhi was released from prison, due to ill health in May, 1944. Nehru and the other political leaders were not released until 15 June 1945.

AFRICA

Government **regulations and prohibitions** increased everywhere in the British colonies. By November 1941 strikes were prohibited in Nigeria, Northern Rhodesia, Hong Kong and the Gold Coast.

The issue of the pay differences between African and European **Medical Officers** in the Colonial Service rumbled on. Someone signing himself 'African' informed the readers of the League of Coloured People's (LCP) *Newsletter* in June 1943 that Colonial Secretary Stanley had argued that salaries for Europeans had to be higher in order to 'attract good Europeans' and that he didn't want 'African Medical Officers to become a privileged class by high salaries'. (p.31) The Fabian Colonial Bureau (FCB) noted in early 1945 that salaries for African medical officers remained at £400 – £720 while Europeans were paid £660 - £1,200; the conditions of service were also unequal. In Tanganyika it was even more uneven: £96 for an African Medical Officer and £800 for a European.[10] This gross inequality applied to all working for the governments (and private companies) at all levels and in all colonies.

A major issue was the use of **forced or 'compulsory' labour** to produce minerals and agricultural products. In early 1942 there were 20,000 forced labourers, aged 16+, working on farms in Kenya. 'Conscripted labour' was then officially approved in Kenya, Tanganyika, Northern Rhodesia, Nigeria, Zanzibar, Sierra Leone and Malta.[11] That some, if not most of this labour was for private companies, and that the workers had 'no safeguards, no accepted conditions of labour', was raised again and again in Parliament in London and reported by the FCB. The Colonial Office and War Office officials responded by saying either that they were going to ask each other, or ask the colonial governors. Then they would report back. In November 1943 the British government avoided replying by giving the Kenyan Executive Council permission to make all decisions.[12]

It was not till November 1945 that the FCB's journal, *Empire,* could report that the Colonial Office was 'consulting with the Governors regarding ending forced labour in private enterprise'. (p.12)

Hansard HC Deb 04 March 1942 vol 378 cc635

KENYA (AFRICAN LABOUR)

Mr. Creech Jones asked the Under-Secretary of State for the Colonies (1) whether African labour in Kenya will be conscripted for use in private European employment; what classes of work Africans will be required to do; whether it is proposed to move Africans from the reserves to work in the European Highlands; whether penal sanctions will operate; what proportion of men will be removed from the native areas; and what arrangements made for their wives and dependants.....

Mr. Harold Macmillan I welcome the opportunity which my hon. Friend has afforded me of making a statement on this subject; but as it is of considerable length I will, with his permission, circulate it in the OFFICIAL REPORT. Following is the statement:

.... It has proved impossible by normal means to secure sufficient labour in Kenya for the increased production campaign which was launched at the request of the Minister of State in Cairo to assist in providing supplies for the Middle East and so save shipping from the United Kingdom or elsewhere.

The Committee has unanimously recommended the introduction of a system of compulsory labour for Africans, of which the principal features will be:—

.... (f) A minimum period of service of 84 days and a maximum period of 12 months.............(g) Penalties: (1) for employers failing to comply with terms or conditions attached to the employment of conscripted Africans; and (2) for employees wilfully failing to comply with the provisions, £5 and/or two months' imprisonment. (The penalty is the same for employers and employees. But it will be appreciated that it is likely that employees would be concerned with only single offences and employers with offences in regard to batches of employees, each of which offences would be punished separately.)

These proposals have been approved by the Secretary of State. It is understood that the immediate shortage of labour for agriculture is in the neighbourhood of 22,500, but it may not be necessary to recruit up to the full extent of the shortage.

Hansard HC Deb 14 April 1943 vol 388 c1204
SIERRA LEONE (CONSCRIPT LABOUR, WAGES)
Mr. David Adams asked the Secretary of State for the Colonies whether he is aware that the shipping companies and dock operating firms of Sierra Leone, having been granted conscript labour for the more efficient working of the port, have refused to pay the increased wages recommended by the Labour Advisory Board some months ago; and whether, as the opportunity for redress of grievances by these workers is limited, he will take steps to ensure the enforcement of such and subsequent recommendations?
Colonel Stanley...... I have no information as to a refusal by the shipping companies and dock operating companies to pay increased wages to civilian labour and am consulting the Governor
Mr. Adams In view of the fact that these workers are conscript labour now, surely the recommendations of the Labour Advisory Board ought to have more weight with the Government than they have? The recommendations are really ignored.
Colonel Stanley As I told the hon. Member on the last occasion, I am finding out from the Governor.

A very serious issue in all the colonies in Africa, and in the West Indies, was the rise in **'cost of living'** which was often double or triple the rare increase in wages. For example, the FCB reported in September 1942 that in West Africa the cost of living had risen an estimated 47%. In Sierra Leone costs had risen by 75%, while the daily wage increased from twelve to fourteen pence, an 18% increase.[13] Official figures were usually disputed by the workers.

West Africa

Africans attempted to protest about their conditions and demand self-determination, if not independence. Those on strike for better wages and conditions were often charged with rioting.

Leaders such as **I.T.A. Wallace-Johnson** of Sierra Leone were imprisoned 'for the duration of the war' according to the FCB.

The **official cost of living index in Lagos**, 100 in 1939, had risen to 170 by July 1945. The workers claimed that in fact it had risen by 200%, with no adequate rise in wages for Africans, while that of Europeans had risen considerably.[14]

The numbers of **'recruited workers'** in **Nigeria** are unavailable. However, as tin production had to be increased after Malaya was lost to the Japanese, 'forced labour was necessary as there were not enough volunteers', the Colonial Under-Secretary of State informed the LCP. There were 100,000 'peasant conscripts' in the tin mines on the Jos Plateau, working in appalling conditions and receiving inadequate food. In response to a question in Parliament, it was stated that in December 1942 there had been 14,098 'conscripted workers' in the mines, out of a total workforce of almost 71,000. Their death rate was c.10%.[15] Their 'scales of wages compared favourably with voluntary labour', the British government maintained. Just what 'favourably' meant was not disclosed.[16]

In Nigeria, low pay, the huge increase in prices, bad working conditions, lack of sick pay/holiday pay/promotion and inequality of wages for Africans and Europeans doing the same job resulted in the formation of a number of trade unions. Strikes were declared illegal in 1942. The most active trade unionist, **Michael Imoudu** (Railway Union) was imprisoned from 1943 until May 1945.[17]

August 1944 saw the formation of the **National Council of Nigeria and Cameroons** (NCNC) which quickly became the leading political/nationalist association in Nigeria. Nnamdi Azikiwe (known as 'Zik') was the General Secretary. In March 1945 the Nigerian Governor, without any consultation, introduced proposals for a new constitution, which gave all land and mineral rights to the Crown. The NCNC protested, as did the workers, angered especially by the Governor's refusal to raise wages. On 1 June, almost a quarter million workers went on strike. The Governor now banned Azikiwe's two newspapers, which supported the strikes.[18]

In 1942 some Africans had been appointed to the Executive Councils in both the Gold Coast and Nigeria. The following year, undoubtedly at least due to the shortage of White workers as so many had been transferred to military duties, the 'Africanisation' of the Administrative service was begun. Governor Burns began to send Gold Coasters 'in the clerical grades to British residential universities to be trained for administrative posts'.[19]

Nnamdi Azikiwe

South and Central Africa

Segregation was ubiquitous in South Africa and in North and South Rhodesia – hosts to European settlers. (There were 13,028 Britons living in Northern Rhodesia (Zambia) in 1931.) Africans were grossly mistreated. The *New Statesman & Nation* reported on 7/12/1940 (p.557) that 17 African workers were killed and 70 injured in a **strike** for better wages at the copper mines there. An African miner's wage was between 9 pence and 14 pence per day while the two major mines announced a profit of £6 million in December 1940.[20]

Empire reported in its March-April 1945 issue that there had been '**labour unrest in Uganda**… regarding the high cost of living and low level of wages… 8 Africans had been killed and 15 wounded…' (p.2)

As the White settlers obtained guaranteed prices for their produce, it is not surprising that a Compulsory Native Labour Recruitment Act was passed in the Rhodesias in 1942. While the European settlers 'obtain excellent prices for their produce', African farmers received about half the prices paid to the Whites.[21]

East Africa

Kenya was also a 'settler' colony: 16,812 Europeans lived there in 1931. **Segregation** was ubiquitous. Africans had been forced off their most productive lands by the British settlers, who then used the Africans as very cheap labour. The wages offered were so low that many Africans refused the jobs offered. This led to a labour shortage, which worsened when the military offered slightly higher wages. In March 1942 a number of MPs in Britain questioned the '22,500 workers aged 16+ "recruited" for agricultural work' in Kenya.[22]

The FCB's *Empire* noted in its September 1941 (p.4) issue that some **Kenyan organisations** had been '**suppressed**' and their leaders jailed. The Colonial Office refused to disclose any information on these events. In May 1943 *Empire* reported that twenty-three members of the Joint Council of Kikuyu Central Organisation and some members of other political organisations had been detained under the Kenya Defence Regulations.[23]

At the end of November 1944 there were 26,032 '**conscripted' workers** in **Kenya**, and 26,256 in **Tanganyika**. A year later, replying to questions in Parliament, the government announced that compulsory labour would be illegal in Kenya and Tanganyika (but not in Northern Rhodesia) from the end of the year.[24]

Empire reported in September 1941 (p.8) that the Kenyan governor had been given '**compulsory recruitment powers**' to assemble Labour Units for the military.

An estimated 35,000 **refugees from Poland** were settled in Britain's East African colonies in camps built for them by Africans. A few thousand were also settled in India.[25]

West Indies

In 1940 there was a Cabinet meeting in London to discuss 'the utilisation of Manpower Resources of the Colonial Empire'. Regarding the West Indies, it was noted that a number of White West Indians were serving in Imperial Forces in the UK. It was thought that 'pioneer (labour) units' were the most suitable, but the 'advantages' of such a formation were 'doubtful'. Thus, despite the need for troops as well as workers, there was very little attempt to recruit in the islands until early 1941 when it was announced that skilled tradesmen could apply at local military headquarters.[26]

In an unsigned article, 'Mobilise the Colonial Empire', in its July 1941 issue, the *Crown Colonist* questioned this policy:

> The West Indies has rendered valuable service by allowing US bases in exchange for 'aid' to the UK. The West Indies have contributed money and men. But why is not much more done to utilize this immense reservoir of active good will? Why, for example, has not that fine corps, with its splendid record of service, the West India Regiment, been reconstituted?

Empire reported in March 1942 (p.8) that the response to a question asked in Parliament regarding this non-recruitment was that it was 'not practicable to raise up West Indian units, but volunteers with special qualifications are encouraged to join British Units'. It was not till late 1944 that technicians/ground crew were recruited for the RAF.

The governors informed the Colonial Office that there was some disquiet on the islands regarding the lack of recruitment when there was so much publicity about the dangers being faced by the 'Mother Country'. For example, there was a public meeting in Port-of-Spain on 4 July 1940 at which a resolution was passed

> to ask His Majesty's Government to use 25,000 men from Trinidad as part of the 250,000 men of the West India corps.... We also feel that it would be most unfair to our Mother Country should we not like our English brothers also taste the horrors of actual warfare.[27]

After years of harassment, in 1939 **Uriah Butler**, one of the workers' leaders in Trinidad,[28] was imprisoned on 'security grounds'. He was released on 11 April 1945. In 1942 Barbados labour leader **Ulric Grant** was imprisoned for ten years for 'sedition'. However, he was released

Uriah Butler

January 1943 and all Bajan trade union leaders were released the following month.[29]

Hansard HC Deb 11 February 1942 vol 377 c1541
BARBADOS (ULRIC GRANT, RELEASE)
Dr. Morgan asked the Under-Secretary of State for the Colonies whether the release from prison last month in the Colony of Barbados of Ulric Grant, a trade union organiser, convicted in 1937 for sedition, was the result of a free pardon granted by the King, or a remission of sentence; and whether it is now proposed to consider the grant of compensation to this man for his unnecessary imprisonment?
Mr. Harold Macmillan Grant was released as the result of a remission of sentence. No question of compensation arises.

Alexander Bustamente, leader of the Bustamente Industrial Trade Union in Jamaica was also imprisoned 'for the duration of the war'. In 1941 three trade union officials and in November 1942 four officials of the Jamaica Government Railway Employees Union were arrested. Nine other unionists were placed under very strict prohibitions/conditions and barred from any public speaking/activities.[30] After considerable pressure from British MPs, in March 1942 Bustamente and by early 1943 most others languishing in prison were released. Bustamente was forbidden to 'attend or address any meetings'.[31]

In 1941 in Jamaica the home of the People's National Party (PNP) leader Norman Manley was raided and his library was confiscated. **W.A. Domingo**, Jamaican activist living in New York, whom Manley had invited to help with the organisation of the PNP, was arrested on his arrival in Kingston. It took protests in the USA and questions in Parliament in 1941 and 1942 for Domingo to be eventually released in February 1943.[32]

As the war progressed, there were **food shortages** on some of the islands and food prices increased, leading to what the _Crown Colonist_ (September 1942, January 1943) called 'hooliganism'.[33] To take the largest island, Jamaica, as an example: in 1941 there were strikes throughout the island for an increase in wages. In 1942 about 30% of the employed population earned less than six shilling a day. The cost of living index, 100 in 1939, was 159 in 1942 – food alone was at 153. The December 1942 Census found 50,528 unemployed aged between 15 and 24.[34] Not surprisingly, though in October 1942 the Governor had made it illegal to belong to a trade union, in 1944 there were 43 **strikes** involving 6,361 workers.[35]

Food rationing was introduced on some islands. In 1944 droughts and then hurricanes worsened the situation. As unemployment was rife, many thousands emigrated to the USA during the war in search of work. As elsewhere, many regulations regarding 'sedition' had been introduced. In Trinidad even Carnival was banned in case it led to some form of protest.[36]

In February 1944 there was a **conference of labour organisations** in Georgetown, British Guiana (Guyana). Their demands included self-government and a political federation of the British colonies, and the confirmation of their rights under the Atlantic Charter.[37]

US military bases had been built on many islands.[38] The influx of US military caused many problems. Thousands of West Indians were employed; though the US refused to negotiate with local trade unions about wages, it did pay more than the pre-war pittance. (The British government did not want higher than normal wages paid.) These new higher wages and the 'free-spending' Americans also led to an increase in prices. The total segregation in the US military and US attempts to impose similar policies also caused problems. For example, there were protests in St.Lucia about the colour bar imposed in bars frequented by Americans. There was more 'disquiet' on the islands when the construction work was finished and the workers were discharged. There was no other work available.[39]

The vast wealth, that is, spending power of the Americans had considerable influence, as sung by calypso singer Lord Invader:

> *Since the Yankees came to Trinidad*
> *They have the young girls going mad,*
> *The young girls say they treat them nice,*
> *And they give them a better price.*
>
> Chorus:
> *They buy rum and Coca-Cola,*
> *Go down to Point Cumana,*
> *Both mother and Daughter*
> *Working for the Yankee dollar.*[40]

— — —

NOTES

1 *Hansard*, 26/6/1940, vol.363, columns 465-90.

2 *About India*, 25 September 1943.

3 A former Marxist, member of the ILP, Solicitor-General (1930) MP (1931) and founder of the Socialist League (1932) Stafford Cripps was expelled from the Labour Party in 1938. Winston Churchill, heading a coalition government, appointed Cripps ambassador to Moscow (May 1940 until January 1942). He then served in the War Cabinet.

4 *Hansard*, 10/9/1942, vol.383, col.304. These murders became world news – reported even in the *Journal of Negro Education*, October 1942 as an 'Editorial Comment'.

5 Gowher Rizvi, *Linlithgow and India: A Study of British Policy and the Political Impasse in India, 1936-1943*, London: Royal Historical Society, 1978, p.125. In his *British Soldier In India: The Letters of Clive Branson* (London: Communist Party, 1944, p.98) Branson notes the arrest of hundreds of Congressmen in Bengal, including 20 members of the Bengal Legislature, in 1942.

6 Jawaharlal Nehru, *The Discovery of India*, London: Meridian Books, 1956, pp.450, 496, 500. (Nehru wrote this in 1944 while imprisoned in Ahmadnagar Fort); *New Statesman & Nation*, 14/12/1940, p.611; Lawrence James, *Raj: The Making and Unmaking of British India*, New York: St. Martin's Press, 1997, p.564. The numbers imprisoned were c. 20,000, according to John Keay, *A History of India*, London: HarperCollins 2000, p.498. *New India* reported in August 1943 that there were 25,000 political prisoners, of whom 11,717 were 'untried' and that the numbers imprisoned increased constantly.

7 The Government stated that under 1,000 had been killed; Congress claimed it was between 4,000 and 10,000. Many government buildings were destroyed. (James [1997 – n.6], p.572) Farwell notes the effects of the censorship. (Byron Farwell, *Armies of the Raj*, London: Viking, 1989, p.310)

8 The 'price index' was 125 in early 1940 and 236 in 1943-4, an almost 90% increase. (H. Pershad, *Indian Taxation During and After WWII*, Bombay: Allied Publishers, 1964, p.43) James (1997 – n.6), pp.578-581; F. Yeats-Brown, *Martial India*, London: Eyre & Spottiswoode, 1945, p.50. For a full account, see Madhusree Mukerjee, *Churchill's Secret War*, Basic Books, 2011; on p.66 she notes that missing archives make it impossible to determine exactly how many people died – or how much food continued to be exported. There is much on the famine in the very interesting collection of letters of a communist British solider serving in India, Clive Branson to his wife (1944 – n.5), from p.85 onwards.

9 James (1997 – n.6), pp.556-7.

10 *Empire*, March-April 1945, p.2. All Medical Officers had received the same training in British medical schools.

11 *Empire*, July 1941; D. Anderson & D. Throup, 'Africans and Agricultural Production in Colonial Kenya', *Jnl. of African History*, 26/4, 1985, pp.327-345.

12 *Empire*, July 1942, p.2 & September 1942, p.8; *War Commentary*, Mid-April, 1942, p.8; see also eg., *Hansard*, 14/4/1943, vol.388, column 1204; *The Times*, 27/11/1943, p.3.

13 *Empire*, May 1942, p.8 & September 1942, p.8. James S. Coleman, *Nigeria: Background to Nationalism*, Benin City: Broburg & Wistrom, 1986, pp.258-9.

14 Coleman (1986 – n.13), pp.258-9.

15 Raymond Dumett, 'Africa's Strategic Minerals During the Second World War, *Jnl. of African History*, 26/4, 1985, pp.381-408; David Killingray, 'Labour Exploitation for Military Campaigns', *Jnl. of Contemporary History*, 24/3, 1989, p.493.

16 LCP *Newletter*, September 1943, pp.145-6; *Empire*, May 1943, p.8; Killingray, (1989 – n.15), p.490. Most of the tin was destined to the UK for armaments. And it must be noted that the British companies in the colonies paid taxes in the UK, not in the colonies.

17 See Baba Oluwide, *Imoudu: A Political History of Nigeria, 1939 – 1950*, Ibadan: Ororo Publications, 1993. (Sadly the index to this very interesting book is totally inaccurate.)

18 Coleman (1986 – n.13), p.264-285. For US interest in the situation in Nigeria, see eg TNA: FO471/44602, correspondence July/August 1945.

19 John Flint, 'Scandal at the Bristol Hotel', *Jnl of Imperial and Commonwealth History*, 12/1, October 1983, p.85.

20 *Empire*, May 1940. £6 million is about £276 million in 2011. In June 1939 Mufulna Mines had announced a profit of £1 million (c. £46 million in 2011) and Roan Antelope Mines £1.3 million (c. £60 million in 2011).

21 Lizzie Collingham, *The Taste of War: World War Two and the Battle for Food*, London: Allen Lane, 2011, pp.132, 135.

22 *War Commentary*, Mid-April, 1942, p.8; *Empire*, March 1942, p.8; *Hansard*, 4, 11, and 26 March 1942. The Secretary of State for the Colonies visited Kenya in 1943 and told the Governor that until the British Government had made a decision about the use of conscripted labour by private companies, no further conscriptions should be undertaken. (27/11/1943, p.3) This was apparently ignored.

23 After the Kenya Central Union was banned, activists formed the Kenya African Study Union, which became the Kenya African Union in 1946. See *Roots of Freedom 1921-1963: the Autobiography of Bildad Kaggia*, Nairobi: East African Publishing House, 1975, p.54.

24 *Empire*, March 1943, p.8, July-August 1945, p.6, January-February 1946, p.9; LCP *Newsletter*, September 1942, pp.139-146.

25 Curtis Abraham, 'When Europeans were refugees in Africa', *New African*, June 2012, pp.72-77; www.dpcamps.org/poland/html. After the war, with the aid of the United Nations Relief and Rehabilitation Administration (UNRRA – established in November 1943) the refugees were re-settled in the UK, Canada and Australia.

26 TNA: CO323/180, files 13117/A, 13117/2 and 13117/10.

27 Ibid, file 13117/16.

28 For a full account, see W. Richard Jacobs (ed), *Butler Versus the King: riots and sedition in 1937*, Port-of-Spain: Key Publications, 1976.

29 *New Leader*, 20 October 1939.

30 *Empire*, April 1940; September 1941, p.6, March 1943, p.6; LCP *Newsletter*, March 1941, p.136; Richard Hart, *Towards Decolonisation*, Kingston: Canoe Press/UWI, 1999, pp.88, 90, 103, 200, 215. (The Railway Union men were Richard Hart, Arthur Henry, Frank Hill and Ken Hill.) For the international protests regarding Domingo's arrest see eg. LCP *Newsletter*, August 1941, p.137.

31 *Empire*, January 1942, p.4, March 1942, p.3.; LCP *Newsletter*, May 1942, p.41; Hart (1999 –n.30), pp. 215, 217; LCP *Newsletter*, September 1941, p.137 & July 1942, p.21; Ken Post, *Strike The Iron: A Colony at War: Jamaica 1939-1945*, Atlantic Highlands, N.J.: Humanities Press, 1981. p.311.

32 Post (1981 – n.31), p.177-179 & 299.

33 This was partly because of the reduction in imports due to U-boat harassment. The result was ever-increasing shortages (and hence rise in prices) of just about everything, as the colonies had not been permitted to manufacture or 'process' anything. They were to serve as the market for British manufactures.

34 The total population was about one and a quarter million.

35 Hart (1999 - n.30), pp.102, 183,189, 284.

36 Albert Gomes, trade unionist, politician, founder of the important magazine *The Beacon*, protested against the banning – and much else. See *Selected Speeches of Albert Gomes*, Port-of-Spain, 1944.

37 *Empire*, May 1944, pp.5-6.

38 It was rumoured that the British government had asked the US not to pay 'above current wages'. (*Empire*, September 1941, pp.4-5, 6)

39 Scott B. MacDonald, *Trinidad & Tobago: Democracy and Development in the Caribbean*, New York: Praeger, 1986, p.65. See also Annette Palmer, 'Black American Soldiers in Trinidad 1942-1944: Wartime Politics in a Colonial Society', *Jnl. of Imperial and Commonwealth History*, 14/3, 1986, pp.203-217; *Empire*, September 1941.pp.4-5. To give just one example of these problems: on 21 April 1943 the Governor of Trinidad telegrammed the British Ambassador in Washington: 'further serious clash between US negro troops and local population'. (TNA: CAB122/1052, file 12/5)

40 From Penny M. Von Eschen, *Race against Empire*, Ithaca: Cornell University Press, 1997, p.37.

CHAPTER 6

THE 'HOME FRONT' IN BRITAIN

The size of the 'Black' population in Britain at the outbreak of WWII is not known. The Census records place of birth, so the many thousands born in Britain cannot be determined. And those listed as born in the colonies would include Whites. There were relatively segregated 'Black'/Indian/Arab communities in Liverpool, Cardiff, South Shields and London. But many, even in these cities, resided among the majority White population.

RACIAL DISCRIMINATION

Ignorance about Africa was profound, and negative attitudes towards Africans ('Black' peoples) were common.[1] This is explained, for example, by D.H. Barber, who became a military officer with the Ugandan Pioneer Corps:

I belonged to a London suburban Sunday School... Sometimes we had missionary talks... I cannot remember ever being given the impression that an African was a human being like myself. He was a soul to be saved... Apart from this Sunday School experience my only knowledge of Africans came from the cinema, where the 'black man' was nearly always a comic figure, with exaggerated emotions and ludicrous fears.[2]

'Colour consciousness' was ubiquitous, as was racial discrimination in many forms, including the use of the 'colour bar'. The level of this 'consciousness' is demonstrated, for example, by the reports in the popular press of the arrival of the first contingent of 'girls' from the West Indies recruited for the Auxiliary Territorial Service. 'Thousands had volunteered', reported the *Evening Standard* (15/10/43) and noted that the recruit photographed 'looked yellow'. The *Evening News* (15/10/1943) said three of the recruits 'looked white'.

When consulted about the proposal to recruit West Indian seamen for the merchant navy, the National Union of Seamen would only agree if they were repatriated after 12 months and if they did not share quarters with the White crew. Perhaps to avoid these restrictions, in September 1941 an agreement was made with the USA to recruit West Indians for ships being built for the UK in the USA. This was curtailed after seven ships had accepted West Indians. On arrival in Britain the men were usually housed in segregated hostels. The British police often registered them as 'aliens', thereby prohibiting them from going ashore.[3]

71

Black Britons (and some colonials who had not been accepted by the military) worked in munitions factories, hospitals – wherever they were accepted. Though some workmates accepted them, 'few pubs or clubs would welcome them'.[4] It was the same in the Air Raid Shelters. Nigerian-born E.I. Ekpenyon, who was trained as an Air Raid Warden in London, reported that 'some shelterers told others to go back to their own countries, and some tried to practise segregation'. Padmore in the *Chicago Defender* (21/10/1939, p.1) reported that 'during the mass evacuation of children from London as air raid precaution measure two Negro children, a boy and a girl, were denied accommodation'. However, not all experienced discrmination: Arjan Baharsing Advani had volunteered for the Auxiliary Fire Service in 1940 and was so highly regarded that the government sent him to India to help with the preparations for the feared invasion by Japan.[5] Dr Baldev Kaushal was awarded an MBE for his 'gallant conduct' in the bombing disaster in Bethnal Green in 1943.[6]

SOME EXAMPLES OF DISCRIMINATION AND USES OF THE 'COLOUR BAR'

1939

As one of the three 'coloured' volunteers in the Paddington (London) Air Raid Precaution (ARP) service had been sacked 'because of his colour', they all resigned. The *Daily Herald* (17/10/1939, p.12) reported that the Commander of the Paddington ARP had told the men 'there is no colour bar here'.
The West African Students Union (WASU) was taking up the case with the Home Secretary and some MPs.

1940

The League of Coloured Peoples reported in its *Newsletters* of August and September that a ship's steward from British Honduras (Belize) had been going to his Labour Exchange for 7 weeks without finding any kind of work. When interviewed by potential employers he was usually told 'we want nothing to do with coloured people'. The level of discrimination was so bad that Ivor Cummings[7] was employed as a Welfare Officer for 'coloured people' by the Colonial Office. Within a few months he was taking up 20 cases of colour discrimination with the Ministry of Labour, as well as the colour bar imposed by the Labour Exchanges for training schemes.

OBITUARY: IVOR CUMMINGS
***The Independent*, 4 December 1992, by Val Wilmer**
Ivor Gustavus Cummings, civil servant, born West Hartlepool 10 December 1913, OBE 1947, died London 17 October 1992.
WHEN the Empire Windrush docked at Tilbury in June 1948, Ivor Cummings was one of the first waiting to greet the initial shipload of Jamaicans arriving to help rebuild war-torn Britain at the government's behest. As a civil servant in the Colonial Office with special responsibilities for Commonwealth citizens, he was there in an official capacity… [During the war] with the arrival of the first Caribbean RAF volunteers, his responsibilities grew, and he travelled widely to combat difficulties arising from racial prejudice. Initially minimal, these increased when the segregated US forces appeared…

In its 25 May issue the *Voice of Ethiopia* (p.1) reported that George Weekes, of West Indian parentage, was applying to the Conscientious Objectors' Tribunal for exemption on 'discrimination grounds' as he had been turned down by both the RAF and the Royal Navy.

1941

The League of Coloured People's (LCP) *Newsletter* reported Harold Moody's extensive correspondence with Colonial Secretary Lord Moyne regarding the colour bar in 'Colonial Administration'. He also took up the many instances of the colour bar from around the UK which had been forwarded to the LCP. The *Newsletter* reported that the government had announced that 'for the duration of the war, conscripted coloured men could be granted commissions'.[8]

Ivor Cummings at a meeting with 'coloured men' from London's East End was told of the colour bar imposed in some air-raid shelters and of harassment by the police. Viscount Cranley, having visited 30 shelters, reported that 'in very few shelters have arrangements been made to divide the coloured population from the white. This division is mutually appreciated and asked for by both white and coloured subjects of this country'.[9]

As some African-American volunteers for both the RAF and for the Medical Service were turned down, the NAACP raised the issue with the British Ambassador. The Ambassador then contacted the Foreign Office, which then contacted various other ministries. A polite response saying absolutely nothing was eventually sent to Washington.[10]

When the USA entered the war, the question of how Britain was to treat African-American troops passing through or stationed in Britain was thoroughly discussed. At first the UK agreed to follow the US segregation policies, but then it changed its mind.

Local newspapers reported incidents of racism against these troops. A White British soldier reported that he had been told 'not to eat or drink with coloured soldiers…just answer their queries and drift away.' An increase in discrimination against Black students in Oxford was also reported.[11]

1942

An important question in the House of Commons evoked the usual evasive response from the Prime Minister. On 29 September

> *Tom Driberg*
> Asked the Prime Minister whether he was aware that an unfortunate result of the presence here of American Forces has been the introduction in some parts of Britain of discrimination against negro troops; and whether he will make friendly representations to the American military authorities asking them to instruct their men that the colour bar is not a custom of this country and that its non-observance by British troops or civilians should be regarded with equanimity?
>
> *Mr Winston Churchill* replied
> The Question is certainly unfortunate. I am hopeful that without any action on my part the points of view of all concerned will be mutually understood and respected.[12]

Was the Bishop of Salisbury the only senior minister in the Church of England to endorse racial discrimination? In an article in the Warminster Parish Magazine he wrote that

> the sharp distinction between white and black across the Atlantic is justified by experience… On no account should young women make acquaintance and take walks with soldiers of African blood.[13]

Kojo-ow Dzifa in a letter published in the *New Statesman* on 20 June argued that

> It is quite evident and urgent that the British people should be educated about their "colonial possessions"… At their best, people regard Africans, whether in uniform or not, as foreigners, who deserve all the petty malevolence they get for being racially different. (pp.405-6)

1943

Some were angry enough to complain: for example, Jamaica-born Napoleon Florent wrote to Ivor Cummings on 29 April 1943, reporting that the Camden Town Labour Exchange for many years had never found him a job. He knew of 'many coloured men who were sent after jobs from labour exchanges, but when they go to the employer, the employer say, "I am sorry but I did not know they were sending us a coloured person", so they did not get the job'. Some years ago, when he applied to the Assistance Board for financial support, he was told to go back to his own country. Now he had applied for the Old Age Pension, but had been told he was not eligible, though he had lived in the UK since 1888.[14]

In 1943 Trinidad-born Learie Constantine, then working for the Ministry of Labour as a Welfare Officer, was booked into the Imperial Hotel in London by the Ministry. The hotel refused to give him a room and called him a 'nigger'. Constantine took the hotel to court, won the case, but only asked for nominal damages'.[15]

IMPERIAL WELCOME

Evening Standard, 7 September 1943

In June, according to the LCP *Newsletter* of August (pp.71-2) Harold Moody received a letter of apology from the War Office regarding the exclusion of applicants of 'non-European descent' for the Imperial Military Nursing Service. 'Steps are being taken to delete it' the War Office assured Moody.

Racial discrimination was so rife, that reports began to appear even in 'mainstream' papers such as the *Daily Dispatch* (7/12/1943) and the *Sunday Pictorial* (19/9/1943). The use of the colour bar to exclude Amelia King, who had volunteered for the Women's Land Army was particularly broadly reported.[16] The Colonial Office turned down the proposal by WASU

Amelia King

and the LCP for an 'Anglo-Colonial Committee' to deal with racism and the colour bar.[17]

1944

Ipswich pubs were refusing to serve African-American soldiers, the *Sunday Pictorial* reported on 22 July. There is an article by George Padmore on the plight of these 'Negro soldiers' in the Jamaican *Sunday Chronicle*, 27/2/1944, p.10. (It is noted that the article is 'censored'.)

Even *The Times* was now reporting racist incidents: on 1 August it reported that George McGuire, a 'coloured' man wearing his Home Guard uniform was refused entrance to a dance hall because of his colour. (p.2). A letter by Harold Moody was published on 10 October (p.8) in *The Times*:

> so numerous are the cases of discrimination brought to our notice...
> The English may be disinclined to bring this matter into the open...
> They will none the less be compelled to do so before long as it is now
> causing a considerable amount of bitterness which may have untoward
> results when this present conflict is over......

There were 350 unemployed 'coloured' seamen in Liverpool and Cardiff in 1944, as the Pool Registrars refused to employ them.[18]

1945

The *News Chronicle* of 16 May reported that a Birmingham hospital, on discovering that a physician just appointed to its staff was a Black man, gave him his notice with a month's salary. He was not allowed to commence work. The Kent Street Baths were put out of bounds to the Black women in the US Women's Auxiliary Army Corps. The LCP *Newsletter* reported in October that

"*We didn't see that notice in the trenches*"

Daily Mirror, 4 September 1943

six Jamaican men serving in the RAF were told by the Auxiliary Territorial Service Commander at a dance in Burton-on-Thames that he was 'averse to the ATS mixing with coloureds'. The August *Newsletter* listed the many forms of the colour bar experienced by serving men. According to the December *Newsletter*, the *Daily Herald* had reported that two Sikhs who had won Victoria Crosses were refused service in a Jermyn St. restaurant in London. 'We don't serve niggers', they were told.

RACISM IN THE MILITARY

1940

The LCP, the International African Service Bureau (IASB) and the West African Students' Union (WASU) all campaigned about racial discrimination in the military. So in October 1939 the government announced that 'British subjects from the colonies and British protected persons in this country' would be eligible for 'emergency commissions in His Majesty's Forces'. But, for example, when Jamaican Dr Leo March responded to the plea for dentists, 'he was refused on the grounds of his 'non-European racial descent'. Black peoples in Britain were refused not only 'commissions': there were reports in the *Daily Herald* (January 11 and February 6) about the refusal of the RAF and the Royal Navy to accept 'Black' volunteers.

The organisations continued their pressure.

Hansard HC Deb 24 January 1940 vol 356 cc562
RECRUITING REGULATIONS.
Mr. Woodburn asked the First Lord of the Admiralty on what grounds George C. Price, of 7, Northfield Square, Edinburgh, born and bred in Edinburgh, was refused entry into the British Navy, in which his British West Indian father fought during the Great War; whether persons born and reared within the British Isles are subject in the recruiting regulations to caste or racial discriminations; and what steps he is taking to abolish colour prejudice in the ranks of the Navy?
Captain Hudson   According to the information available at the Admiralty, George C. Price has never applied to join the Royal Navy. During the war men of colour may be considered for entry for hostilities only service in competition with other candidates on their merits, and without regard to their colour, provided they are British born and sons of British born parents….. I understand that this is rather an extraordinary case. The man's mother is Danish. Therefore he is not the son of British-born parents

1942

The War Office conceded – to a very limited extent - in 1942. Dr. Harold Moody's two medically qualified children, Harold and Christine were accepted by the Army's Medical Corps, as was Dr. Leo March.[19] How the *African* medical officers fared is questionable, as the LCP's *Newsletter* reported in March 1945 that the salary of African Medical Officers (MO) in Tanganyika was £96 while that of a European MO was £600. Dr. Moody's son Arundel became the first Black officer recruit: he was admitted to the Officers' Training Corps, served in the West Kent Regiment and in 1945, promoted to the rank of Major, was posted to the Caribbean Regiment. Garth Moody was accepted for training by the RAF.[20] It has not been possible to discover whether any other Black Britons were accepted.

Moody also raised the issue of flogging used by the military in West Africa. The War Office did not deny its use; it just pointed out that flogging had to be approved by the General Court Martial.[21]

1943

The Admiralty's Recruitment Regulations of 6 March stated that 'black and coloured men and boys and any person in whom there is evidence of such parentage or ancestry, unless with the special sanction of the Admiralty, are absolutely ineligible for entry'.[22]

1944

In February an official in the Foreign Office noted in an internal memo that

> no-one dare admit officially (what is the fact) that coloured persons are nearly always turned down by the Service departments... while we must keep up the fiction that there is no colour bar, only those with special qualifications are likely to be accepted.[23]

The address by a Royal Navy captain to 'white naval recruits' was reported by the *Daily Herald* on 17 May (p.2):

> Although the black soldiers are a very useful addition to our war effort, their presence certainly raises a problem. So that there can be no friction in the manner of dealing with them, I want your standards to conform as near as possible to those of our American Allies. In the States Negroes are separated from the white men. The American regards the Negro as a child and not as an equal to the white race. Please conform to that idea.

The question of whether African troops could be flogged was raised in Parliament again a number of times, without eliciting a firm response. The questioning continued, without ever receiving anything but an evasive response.[24]

1945

Questions were asked in Parliament about pay and allowances for African troops and their treatment while in India en route to the Burma campaign. Responses from the government were, as always, evasive.[25]

The February LCP *Newsletter* (p.19) printed a letter from a West Indian serving in the RAF: why weren't West Indians serving in Britain paid 'overseas pay', when Englishmen serving in the West Indies received this, he asked.

Why did their wives receive one-third of the allowance paid to the wives of Englishmen?

In June Reginald Sorensen MP again questioned the use of whipping in the African armies. The post-war Labour Government announced in April 1946 that it was banned.

1946

Questioning in Parliament continued. After asking many times for the removal of the colour bar in the military, on 2 April MP Major Wilkes was told 'all British subjects, without distinction of colour or descent, are now equally eligible for the Royal Air Force'. On 9 April Gallagher asked the Secretary of State for War if Sandhurst Military Academy was retaining its exclusion of anyone not the son of 'British subjects and of pure European descent'. He was told to refer to the answer given to Major Wilkes. This, of course, only removed the colour bar in the RAF. On 5 November Tom Driberg queried an advertisement stating that all applicants for engineering cadetships in the military must be of 'pure European descent'. He was told that 'The stipulation referred to applies to all entrants into the Regular Army for general service'.

1947

In 1947 the Cabinet finally decided that 'British subjects of non-European descent should be admitted to the Royal Navy and the British Army, provided they attained the requisite standard, were resident in this country and could satisfy the selection authorities that they were likely to mix with other entrants and hold their own in the corporate life of the Services'.[26] This, of course, made it quite easy for 'coloured' applicants to be rejected.

POLITICAL ACTIVITIES IN BRITAIN

Activists – and journalists - had to be very careful in order to avoid imprisonment for 'sedition' or have their publications banned.

1940

The Anti-Slavery and Aborigines Protection Society issued a Manifesto, 'Native Races, the War and Peace Aims' in March. This began by acknowledging that 'colonial territories' might be affected

> by considerations of international politics once the war was over. Racial
> discrimination had been spreading in Africa, barring members of native
> races from positions where they might influence policy... The question
> of self-government must be taken far more seriously than in the past.

There were strikes by Lascar seamen in a number of ports, protesting at the ongoing inequality in the War Bonus. White seamen received £10 while others received £3 per month. A number of strikers were imprisoned.[27]

1941

The National Council for Civil Liberties held a Delegate Conference on 'Civil Liberty in the Colonial Empire' on 15th and 16th February. Krishna Menon of the India League was one of the speakers. The LCP attended. The agreed Resolution stated: 'We view with serious concern the lack of civil liberties in territories under British colonial administration'.[28]

Arthur Creech Jones, MP had an article 'The prisoners of our Empire', printed in the *Tribune*, 22nd August. He questioned the many imprisoned without trial, emphasising that the powers of the colonial governors threatened civil liberties. But he did not question other 'civil liberty' issues in the colonies.

In August Menon organised a conference to demand the release of Jawaharlal Nehru from prison and to discuss the 'issue of freedom'. The following month the India League held a two-day conference: it demanded negotiations with Britain based on the Atlantic Charter.[29] When the League of Coloured Peoples asked Winston Churchill to clarify the meaning of the Charter; he replied that 'no fresh statement is needed'.[30]

1942

To get support for its campaigns against the many forms of racial discrimination and for colonial independence, the West African Students Union established a West African Parliamentary Committee, to act as a pressure group. It was chaired by Reginald Sorensen MP. At its Annual General Meeting the Union demanded immediate self-government and independence within five years of the end of the war.

Responding to a request by British Guiana-born musician/journalist Rudolph Dunbar, the Minister of Information wrote an article for publication in the *Sunday Express,* entitled 'Colour bar must go'. Much of what he wrote in September 1942 is still relevant today, seventy years later:

> There is, of course, no legal Colour Bar in this country... Coloured people in Britain come from the British colonies. They are therefore British citizens with, in theory, the same rights as any Englishman... But it is in fact true that there is still some colour prejudice in this country and still social barriers against coloured people... Few people in this country know anything about black men... No Act of parliament can remedy this. Removing the misconceptions and prejudices which rise is

therefore largely a question of education... Those who still have a prejudice against colour will be taught in time to overcome it... But the existence of a social colour bar is not due entirely to ignorance. It is also due to the ancient insularity of the British people... The barriers still standing in the way of the social equality of coloured peoples must be withdrawn.

Defender Scribe Wins British Censor Fight

By GEORGE PADMORE
(Chicago Defender London Correspondent)

LONDON. — A parliamentary storm which broke as a result of censorship of this correspondent's dispatch reporting the strongest official statement which has yet been made on the color bar has finally forced its release.

Some weeks ago, the British Minister of Information, the Rt. Hon. Mr. Brendan Bracken, writing in Lord Beaverbrooks' "Sunday Express," said in the course of his article, "The barriers still-standing in the way of the social equality of colored people must be withdrawn. The people must be taught by precept and example to overcome their prejudices. This is a process which will take time, but responsible people in Britain are determined that it shall be carried through, the sooner the better."

A cable was immediately filed by this correspondent showing the significance of this pronouncement. It was withheld by the censor who refused to allow it to be sent to the Chicago Defender. Journalists and newspaper correspondents, here in London, were indignant and protested that it was the worst piece of censorship they had yet come up against.

Anxious about the freedom of the press, Mr. Fred Ballenger, a socialist member of parliament, raised the matter in the House of Commons. He asked the Minister of Information if it were true that his article entitled, "The Color Bar Must Go," which was released for the colonies was denied to the Chicago Defender.

Mr. Bracken pointed out that he personally was not responsible for the censorship but that one of the officials in his office with mistaken zeal had ordered it. This official had taken the position that this dispatch might be connected with the arrival of American Negro troops in England, and might seem to be a piece of gratuitous advice to one of Britain's Allies on how to deal with their citizens.

Mr. Bellenger then asked, "Do I understand that this article with those lofty sentiments with which I entirely agree, will now be released .or publication in any other part of the world if so desired?"

To which Mr. Bracken replied, "Yes sir. Any paper that likes to publish this dully written collection of trisms is quite welcome to do so."

Regardless of how much the official British government tries to play down this statement it is of extreme importance to the Negro peoples of the world including those in the United States. For it is a clear cut declaration of British policy in regards to the question of color.

In this article Mr. Bracken also said, "But the existence of the color bar in this country is not entirely due to ignorance. It is also due to the ancient insularity of the British people . . . Fortunately we are a practical people, not unamenable to the pressure of events. There was a time when Englishmen, looked upon Scotsmen, Irishmen and Welshmen as foreigners, and long after they ceased constitutionally to be foreigners they were still regarded as somehow alien. But the English learned to overcome this prejudice in time. Certainly it is the desire of the British government that this prejudice (against blacks) should go."

Chicago Defender, 21 November 1942

1943

In 1943 the Fabian Colonial Bureau held a conference, chaired by Harold Moody, regarding the Atlantic Charter. The resolutions demanded that 'coloured people' should be included in the Charter, and responsible government be given at the 'earliest possible moment'. 'All forms of economic exploitation' should be ended.[31]

The LCP's proposed 'Charter for Colonial Freedom' was discussed at its Annual General Meeting. It was agreed that 'the freedoms of the Atlantic

Charter should be the basis of the administration of all colonies'. Philip Noel-Baker MP, the chair of the LCP's Executive, is reported as having 'welcomed the resolution as it established the principle that the government of backward peoples was a trust exercised by the ruling nations for the world at large'. The Charter was circulated widely within the UK, the USA and to Nigeria.[32]

WASU sent a letter to the Colonial Secretary asking for 'internal responsible self-government now (for the colonies in Africa)… make the Atlantic Charter directly applicable to them'.[33]

On the last day of its conference, when the 'Executive Table was almost empty', the Labour Party discussed its policy towards colonies and decided that 'it supported the demand that the four freedoms of the Atlantic Charter should be the basis for the administration of all the colonies'.[34]

Indians in Glasgow raised £3,000 for the relief of the famine in Bengal.[35] The India League published leaflets and held meetings to explain and to support the Quit India movement, and to publicise and raise funds for the famine.[36]

Nnamdi Azikiwe, Nigerian political activist and editor of the *West African Pilot*, led the eight West African journalists invited on a 'goodwill tour' of the UK. He addressed a meeting at WASU, and many others, on the application of the Atlantic Charter to West African colonies. British and French colonies should be united into a 'West Africa ruled by Africans', he argued. Azikiwe submitted a Memorandum, 'The Atlantic Charter and British West Africa', to the Secretary of State for the Colonies. Among its demands were immediate internal self-government for the next ten years, followed by five years of full self-government, and then total independence. The British government did not even bother to reply. The delegation was refused accommodation by some hotels.[37]

1944

In January the LCP *Newsletter* reported that it had written to Jan Smuts, Prime Minister of South Africa, asking for his assurance 'that the policy of segregation will no longer be pursued and that everything will be done in the most active manner possible to raise the standard of the African peoples in the Union to one of equality with the Europeans therein'.

In July the LCP held its regular two-day Annual General Meeting. Having received comments, the LCP now finalised its 'Charter for Coloured Peoples' to send to the about-to-be-formed United Nations Organisation (UNO). The Charter called for

1. The elimination of all racial discrimination;
2. The same economic, educational, legal, and political rights for all persons, male and female whatever their colour;

3. A definite time schedule for economic, educational, social and political development in all colonies;
5. Economic development must be 'in the interest of the peoples of the regions concerned';
6. The educational plans must prepare peoples 'in the shortest possible time to play their full part in all spheres and at all levels of activity in their own countries';
7. Indigenous peoples must immediately have 'a majority of all law-making bodies and shall be granted full self-government at the earliest possible opportunity';
8. Imperial powers 'shall be required to account for their administration of dependent territories to an international body'.

Dr Moody sent a copy of the Charter to the government, and to the Phelps Stokes Fund in the USA, which had its own Africa, War and Peace Aims Committee. Moody advised that the government

> had expressed favourable opinions though up to the present time they do not seem to be willing to adopt it as an instrument of policy'. [He was] anxious to secure the opinion of the American Government... [The Charter] could play a major part in helping to shape the future policy of our peoples when the United Nations settle down to frame the peace.

Could the Fund help? Anson Phelps Stokes replied that the education programs would have to be strengthened prior to implementation as in 'large areas of Africa there are no educated people...or Africans with experience'.[38]

The LCP set up a committee to 'survey the colour question in some aspects of English education'. The five researchers scrutinised the content of school text books and teaching practices. Books were found to either present nothing or to present information about 'native peoples' that was grossly biased and 'conveyed prejudice against coloured people'. Teachers were untrained to teach anything about the Empire and its peoples. The report was published as *Race Relations and The Schools*. Much of it is relevant to the school curricula, the training of teachers and school texts today.

1945, January to May

After Hitler's suicide the Axis Powers in Europe surrendered on 8 May 1945.

At its AGM the LCP produced a manifesto, 'Africa in the Post-War World', which it intended to send to the forthcoming UNO meeting in San Francisco. It was presented about mid-May – and ignored.[39]

A number of trade unionists from the colonies attended the World Federation of Trade Unions' initial meeting in January. The conference issued a Manifesto, *Call to All Peoples*, demanding that the terms of the Atlantic Charter should be applied to all colonies.[40]

The League of Coloured Peoples

(Founder and President: HAROLD A. MOODY, M.D., B.S. Lond.)

General & Travelling Secretary · · SAMSON MORRIS
Assistant Secretary · · · · Mrs. MARGARET FULLER
Hon. Acting Treasurer · · · Miss JOAN E. MOODY
Hon. Treasurer · · Capt. C. O. MOODY, R.A.M.C. (On Service)

Communications to:
THE LEAGUE OF COLOURED PEOPLES,
19, OLD QUEEN STREET,
WESTMINSTER, S.W.1.

Phone: Cables:
WIIItehall 6591.   Amorpeck, London.

MANIFESTO ON

AFRICA IN THE POST-WAR WORLD

FOR PRESENTATION TO THE UNITED NATIONS CONFERENCE, SAN FRANCISCO, APRIL 1945.

Promulgated and supported by

The League of Coloured Peoples

in co-operation with

West African Students' Union (London),

International African Service Bureau, (London),

Negro Association (Manchester),

Negro Welfare Centre (Liverpool and Manchester),

Coloured Men's Institute (East London),

and endorsed by the following Colonial Trade Union Leaders on behalf of their unions:

J. S. Annan, Gold Coast Trade Unions.

T. A. Bankole, President, Nigerian T.U.C.

H. N. Critchlow, British Guiana Trade Unions

J. A. Garba-Jahumpa, Secretary Gambia T.U.C.

NOTES

1   See, eg Marika Sherwood, 'Sins of omission and commission: history in English schools and struggles for change', *Multicultural Teaching*, Spring 1998 and 'Race, Empire and Education: teaching racism', *Race & Class*, 42/3, 2001, and also 'In this curriculum I don't exist', www.history.ac.uk/education (2005). Some early books outlining racial discrimination are: Douglas Lorimer, *Colour, Class and the Victorians*, Leicester University Press, 1978; Anthony Richmond, *Colour Prejudice in Britain*, London: Routledge & Kegan Paul, 1954; Bob Hepple, *Race, Jobs and the Law in Britain*, London: Allen Lane, 1968; E.J.B. Rose, *Colour and Citizenship*, OUP, and IRR, 1969.

2   D.H. Barber, *Africans in Khaki*, London: Edinburgh Press, 1948, p.vii.

3   Marika Sherwood, *Many Struggles: West Indian Workers and Service Personnel in Britain 1939-1945*, London: Karia Press, 1985, pp.134-5, and 'Lascar Struggles against discrimination in Britain 1923-1945: the work of N.J. Upadhyaya and Surat Alley', *The Mariner's Mirror*, 90/4, 2004. On Arab seamen in Britain, see Richard Lawless, *From Ta'izz to Tyneside*, University of Exeter Press, 1995.

4   From David Bygott, quoted by Stephen Bourne, 'We also served', *BBC History Magazine*, September 2000, pp. 46-8.

5   E.I. Ekpenyon, *Some Experiences of an African Air-Raid Warden*, London: Sheldon Press, c.1945, p.10. See also the journal *West Africa* (28/10/39) for dismissals/non-acceptance in the ARP. Peter Fryer lists the 'Black' ARP wardens, and other war workers he could locate. (*Staying Power*, Pluto Press, 1984, p. 331) 'Arjan Baharsing Advani', *ASACACHIB Newsletter*, #10, Sept. 1994, p.12.

6   Email from Dr Florian Stadtler, 30 August 2012.

7   Cummings' father was a Sierra Leone medical student in Britain and his mother was a White nurse; the father returned to Freetown to practise. Sadly, there are no biographies of this very interesting and committed man.

8   There is much on this in the CO323 series at the National Archives. (TNA)

9   Stephen Bourne, *Mother Country: Britain's Black Community on the Home Front 1939-45*, Stroud: History Press, 2010, pp. 26-7; *Sunday Times*, 5/1/1941, p.7.

10 TNA: FO371/26205 & /30665; copious correspondence October 1941 – February 1942. How it was to be handled is indicated by this comment from a Military Attaché: 'Due to political attitudes re black and white equality, we shall be forced to say OK, even though eventually we take none'. (TNA: FO371/26226) See Marika Sherwood, 'Walter White and the British: a lost opportunity', *Contributions to Black Studies*, Nos. 9/10, 1990-1992, pp. 215-226. NAACP = National Association for the Advancement of Coloured People, founded in the USA in 1909.

11 *New Statesman*, 22/8/1943, p.121, 'London Diary'. See eg., *Afro-American*, 21/11/1942, p.3; *Bristol Evening World*, 23/7/1942, p.2; *Evening Standard*, 29/8/1942; *Daily Herald*, 7/7/1942 & 22/9/1942, p.2; *New Leader*, 26/9/1942; *Times*, 2/10/1942. For a full account of African-American troops' experiences, see Graham Smith, *When Jim Crow met John Bull*, London: I B Tauris, 1987.

See also *Picture Post*, 17/7/1943 and Janet Toole, 'GIs and the race bar in wartime Warrington', *History Today*, July 1994, pp.22-28.

12 This was reported in the *Evening Standard* on 29 September 1942. See also letter in *New Statesman and Nation* (22 August 1942, p.121) by a 'British soldier' reporting that 'in an English port part of a well known restaurant is barred to coloured troops'.

13 *Daily Herald*, 22/9/1942, p.2.

14 TNA: CO981/17. In the same file is Florent's complaint to the Colonial Secretary about racial discrimination in Brixton in 1948.

15 *The Times*, 20/6/1944. See Learie Constantine, *Colour Bar*, London: Stanley Paul, 1954; Bourne (2010 – n.9), pp.31-5.

16 *Daily Worker*, 24/9/1943; *News Chronicle*, 24 & 25/9/1943.

17 Hakim Adi, *West Africans in Britain 1900 – 1960*, London: Lawrence & Wishart, 1998, p.108.

18 Sherwood (1985 – n.3), p.136. McGuire's exclusion from the dance hall was reported in *West Africa*, 12/8/1944.

19 LCP *Newsletter* August 1942, p.127.

20 *The Guardian*, 12/2/1940; TNA: CO323/1692/4, file 7213/2, internal memo. Email from David Killingray, 10/2/2012.

21 LCP *Newsletter*, September 1942, p.149 & May 1944. In the books/reports I have read there is no indication that flogging needed such approval. Nominally it was banned in 1941, but the CO announced in 1944 that it was retained.

22 Quoted in Marika Sherwood, 'Blacks in the Royal Navy', *BASA Newsletter*, #23, January 1999, pp.13-15.

23 TNA: FO371/43005.

24 *Hansard*, 19/4/1944, vol.399, col. 190-91; 11/4/1945, vol. 409, col.1833; 21/8/1945, vol. 413, col.467; 27/2/1946, vol.419, col.392; 5/6/1946, vol.423, col.329. Flogging had been abolished in the British Army in the 19th century.

25 *Hansard*, 28/2/1945, vol.408, col. 1414.

26 *Times*, 5/6/1947, p.8; TNA: CAB128/10, quoted in Sherwood (1985 – n.3), p.25. (There is a relatively full account of the endless discussion on this by various government departments in this book, pp.3-25.)

27 Marika Sherwood, 'Lascars in Glasgow and the West of Scotland during World War II', *Scottish Labour History*, 38, 2003, pp.37-50.

28 *The Guardian*, 17/2/1941; LCP *Newsletter*, March 1941, p.135. Menon served as an air-raid warden in St.Pancras, London, during the war. On the history of Indians in Britain, see Rozina Visram, *Asians in Britain*, London: Pluto Press, 2002; Kusoom Vadgama, *India in Britain*, London: Robert Royce, 1984.

29 On the Charter, see Chapter 7. See also K.C. Arora, *Indian Nationalist Movement in Britain (1930 – 1949)*, New Delhi: Inter-India Publications, 1992.

30 Visram (2007 – n.28), pp. 334-5; LCP *Newsletter*, December 1941, p.26.

31 LCP *Newsletter*, February 1943, p.149.

32 LCP *Newsletter*, April. 1943, p.3; *Daily Herald*, 19/6/1943. See Marika Sherwood, '"Diplomatic Platitudes": The Atlantic Charter, the United Nations and Colonial Independence', *Immigrants & Minorities*, 15/2, 1996, pp.135-150; esp. pp.138-

139. Given this statement, some might question why Philip Noel-Baker held such a position at the LCP.

33 Adi (1998 – n.17), p.107.

34 TNA: CO323/1858 (9050/3, 1943), which quotes the *Daily Herald* of 19/6/1943 and also the *Crown Colonist*.

35 Sherwood (2003 – n.27), p.38.

36 Visram (2002 - n.28), p.336; on the surveillance of Menon and attempts to counteract his propaganda, see pp.337-9.

37 LCP *Newsletter*, June 1943, p.64 & September-October 1943, p.87. The Memorandum is reproduced in full in *African Interpreter*, 1943. TNA: CO554/133 notes that Zik's luggage was searched but 'nothing of interest was found'; James S. Coleman, *Nigeria: Background to Nationalism*, Benin City: Broberg & Wintrom, 1986, pp.240-41. On Zik, see eg., M.S.O. Olisa & O.M. Ikejiani-Clark, *Azikiwe and the African Revolution*, Lagos: Africana-FEP Publishers, 1989.

38 Schomburg Center: Phelps Stokes Papers, Box 40, file 17, Moody to PS Fund 26/9/1944 and Anson Phelps Stokes to Moody, 21/10/1944; report in LCP *Newsletter*, September 1944, p.86.

39 LCP *Newsletter*, April 1945, pp.9-13; Sherwood (1996 – n.32).

40 Marika Sherwood, 'The United Nations: Caribbean and African-American Attempts to Influence the Founding Conference in San Francisco in 1945', *Jnl. of Caribbean History*, 29/1, 1995, pp. 27-58.

SECTION 4

INTERNATIONAL INTERESTS IN THE COLONIES

This Section looks briefly at the interests of the USA and then at the formation of the United Nations. The American-built bases on British 'owned' Caribbean islands and in Britain's West African colonies has been discussed in Chapter 3.

The US always avowed that it was against imperialism. However, some would argue that imperialism does not necessarily mean *direct* control. It could mean the influence / control of politicians, and / or control of the economy. Prior to WWII, the US faced a 'problem' with the colonies of the European powers, who usually only permitted *exports* to the USA, by their own trading companies and shipping lines.[1]

I have not dealt with the discussions between the colonial powers, especially the UK and France after WWII, regarding the future of their colonial 'possessions'.

The influence of the League of Nations, founded after WWI, declined with the emergence of what became known as the Axis Powers – Germany, Italy, Japan. Winston Churchill and Franklin D. Roosevelt met in 1941 and signed the Atlantic Charter, on which they based their co-operation against the Axis. This became the foundation of further discussions, eventually including the USSR. Fifty-one nations met in San Francisco, California in 1945 to debate and sign the Charter of the United Nations.

CHAPTER 7

AMERCIAN INTEREST IN THE COLONIES

That the USA was very interested in British colonies was noted, for example, in an article in *The Sunday Times* of 29 December 1940: 'America and the War', written by S.E. Thomason, the proprietor of the *Chicago Daily Times*:

> Most of those whose opinion I can learn still feel that our recognition of your need for armaments and our help in providing them, should be met with an offer to transfer your Caribbean insular possessions in exchange.

As the US edged closer to participating in what was then a European conflict, one thing President Franklin Delano Roosevelt was positive about was that the US would not help Britain 'simply so that she will be able to continue to ride roughshod over colonial peoples'.[2] The US Ambassador to Britain emphasised that 'there was no subject on which a greater divergence of viewpoint existed between (the US and the UK) than British colonial policy'.[3] However, the President was interested in the British Empire not only for altruistic reasons: the US had been excluded from the empires' trade and raw materials by all the imperial powers. Thus the US continued to press Britain over the issue of colonial emancipation, especially India, throughout the war.[4]

In March 1941 the UK and the USA signed what became known as the **Lend Lease Act**. This promised a vast supply of armaments and foodstuffs to Britain and her allies; repayment would 'not be in money but by returning the goods or using them in support of the cause, or by a similar transfer of goods'. The Act was also used to further American free trade policies: the negotiations in 1942 'included requirements for the United Kingdom to open its empire to free trade'. Lend Lease was not extended into the postwar period.[5]

Prime Minister Winston Churchill and President Roosevelt met in August 1941 on board the USS *Augusta* off Newfoundland, to discuss the war situation. After three days of deliberations they announced 'certain common principles' - these came to be known as the Atlantic Charter.[6] The third clause of the Charter stated that the two men 'respect the right of all peoples to choose the form of government under which they will live; and they wish to see sovereign rights and self-government restored to those who have been forcibly deprived of them'.[7]

At a conference held in September 1941 the Allied Governments endorsed the Atlantic Charter. But to whom this third clause applied immediately became a contentious issue. 'Both the President and I', wrote US Secretary of State Cordell Hull, 'repeatedly said the Atlantic Charter (was) applicable to all such (dependent) peoples throughout the world... Prime Minister Churchill repeatedly maintained that Point Three of the Charter (the right to self-determination) applied only to the occupied countries of Europe.' At the Lord Mayor's Luncheon, on 10 November 1942 (and elsewhere) Churchill asserted that 'I have not become the King's First Minister in order to preside over the liquidation of the British Empire'.[8]

'a fishing trip'. *Guardian*, 15 August 1941

On December 7, 1941 Japan bombed the American naval base at Pearl Harbour, Hawaii. Four days later Hitler declared war on the United States. The USA was now in the war.

Towards the end of 1942, Wendell Willkie, then an informal ambassador of President Roosevelt, argued that the colonial people's support in the war could only be gained if a

firm time-table [was set up] under which they can work out and train up the government of their own choosing... Freedom means orderly and scheduled abolition of the colonial system... As Americans we must also recognise that we share with these men and women of the British Commonwealth of free nations the responsibility of making the whole world a Commonwealth of Free Nations.

Colonies had 'eventually' to attain their freedom, 'otherwise they might get what they want via a war'.[9]

In Europe, especially in the UK, there was much suspicion of the interests of the USA.[10] The Department of State's 'Africa expert', Henry Villard attempted to allay such fears. As instant independence would lead to chaos, he proposed

international trusteeship over the enemy's colonies... An open door trade policy to make raw materials available to all was one of the major reasons for conquests... The USA has no designs on the colonial posses-sions of other nations and no desire to carve out for its exclusive benefit any portion of Africa.

George Padmore explained that

American Big Business does not seem anxious to acquire political control of colonies... Dollar diplomacy can secure the United States all the advantages it seeks without the responsibilities of policing overseas territories... America will emerge from this war the greatest imperial-ist nation...and as such, Britain's chief commercial competitor for the markets of the world... The covert struggle between Britain and America for imperial mastery is being pushed more and more into the open... England without an Empire would be merely a geographical expression, an insignificant island of 46 million people off the fringe of Western Europe.[11]

He repeated this argument in a number of articles and pointed out that 'wider markets are an absolute necessity for US capitalism'.[12]

Naturally organisations in Britain wanted to exploit the Atlantic Charter in their struggles for the colonies' independence. In August 1941 Clement Attlee, then Leader of the Opposition in Parliament, advised students at a WASU conference that 'the Atlantic Charter will apply to coloured people'. A month later, on September 13, the League of Coloured Peoples wrote to Prime Minister Churchill arguing that the

principles which underlie freedom are the same for Africans and Asians as for Europeans... We would like to feel assured that the freedom which you seek for Europeans and Britons is exactly the same freedom that you seek for the loyal inhabitants of the many Colonies of the British Empire.

Churchill replied that 'no fresh statement was needed as he had already declared the policy for the British Empire'. Churchill had announced in Parliament on 9 September that 'at the Atlantic meeting, we had in mind, primarily, the restoration of the sovereignty, self-government and national life of the States and nations of Europe now under the Nazi yoke'. He constantly re-iterated that there could be 'no question of our being hustled or reduced into any declaration affecting British sovereignty in any of our Dominions or Colonies'.[13]

In the USA Nwafor Orizu, speaking on the radio on 16 August 1942 in Ohio where he was a student, stated that

> The problem of African Countries is that they want to know now whether the Christian nations are really ready to apply the Atlantic Charter to all the world who shed their blood in this war. Nigerian Press has already communicated with the Prime Minister of Great Britain on this issue...[14]

AMERICA IN THE CARIBBEAN

In 1941 the British government agreed to American proposals to set up the **Anglo-American Caribbean Commission** (AAPC). Almost immediately the Jamaica's People's National Party (PNP) protested about the lack of representation by the peoples of the islands. The Colonial Office was alarmed, noting that 'certain members had a tendency to magnify the scope of the Commission, in fact, to contemplate an executive organisation'. So the CO asked the Foreign Office to 'apply through the Embassy a gentle pressure of the brake on US enthusiasm'. But the USA had a good excuse: Under-Secretary of State Sumner Welles had advised the Foreign Office on 10 April 1941 that economic conditions in the West Indies are likely to become difficult... negro organisations in New York are likely to become troublesome in that event'.[15]

The Commission had been officially established in March 1942 after considerable discussion. It was chaired by Charles Taussig, an American merchant/ politician, close to President Roosevelt and with interests in the Caribbean sugar industry. It had a very strong advisory role: America wanted to strengthen social and economic co-operation in the area. In 1944 Trinidadian Eric Williams, teaching at Howard University in Washington DC at the time, was appointed as a researcher to the Commission by Taussig.[16]

— — —

American and West Indian Negroes Unite - to
EXTEND OUR MUTUAL RIGHTS
In the West Indies and Right here in the U. S.
MONSTER
MASS MEETING

SUNDAY, APRIL 26, 1942 — 3 p. m.

AT RENAISSANCE CASINO (GOOD OLD RENNIE)
Corner 138th Street & 7th Avenue   New York City

Come and Join with

Prominent American and West Indian Speakers

In

Demanding Greater Negro Representation

On

The Anglo-American Caribbean Commission
& The Caribbean Advisory Committee

and

In Seeking U. S. Government Aid
for Improving Conditions in the West Indies

Chairman: Dr. LUCIEN M. BROWN

Among the invited and expected Speakers are:
Rev. Dr. A. CLAYTON POWELL, Jr., Councilman   Dr. LUCIEN M. BROWN
Rev. Dr. J. HERMAN ROBINSON   Mr. HODGE KIRNON
ATTY. JOSEPH C. MORRIS

SHORT MUSICAL PROGRAM — SHORT SPEECHES

Auspices of

American-West Indian Negro Committee on Caribbean Affairs
Dr. LUCIEN M. BROWN   I. NEWTON BRAITHWAITE
Chairman   Secretary

Notes

1 On Britain's relationship with the USA, especially regarding colonies, see, eg., Peter Clarke, *The Last Thousand Days of the British Empire*, New York: Bloomsbury Press, 2008; Wm. Roger Louis, *Imperialism at Bay*, New York; Oxford University Press, 1978. See also the very interesting account by Communist author R. Palme Dutt, *Britain's Crisis of Empire*, London: Lawrence & Wishart, 1949.

2 Elliott Roosevelt, *As He Saw It*, New York, 1946, p.25.

3 *The Times*, 1/8/1942, p.5.

4 See, eg., W. Roger Louis, 'American Anti-colonialism and the British Empire', *International Affairs*, 81/3, Summer 1965, pp.397 – 420. The Foreign Office was well aware of this, as attested by an internal Memo on November 1940: 'real US aim is hegemony'. (TNA: FO371/24263) See also TNA: CO318/452/Box & files 71265CO318/453. On some of the UK Cabinet discussions on pressures from the USA, see TNA: CAB 123/239, file 178 and CAB122/1035, file 11/21.

5 *Warren F. Kimbal*, 'Lend-Lease Act (1941)', www.enotes.com › Law and Politics. When the US terminated the Lend Lease in August 1945, to avert bankruptcy Britain was forced to ask for a huge loan - $4.34bn (c. US$56 billion in 2012). It was finally repaid in December 2006. (*Independent*, 29/2/2006)

6 See Marika Sherwood, '"Diplomatic Platitudes": The Atlantic Charter, the United Nations and Colonial Independence', *Immigrants & Minorities*, 15/2, July 1996, pp.135-150. For a summary of the relationship of Roosevelt with Churchill, and the years before the USA entered the war, see Deter Perkins, *The New Age of Franklin Roosevelt, 1932-45*, University of Chicago Press,1957, chapters 4, 5 and 7. Their correspondence, in 3 volumes, was published by Princeton University Press in 1984.

7 On the signing of the Atlantic Charter and its text, see the accounts by the journalist H.V. Morton, *Atlantic Meeting*, Methuen & Co, London 1943 and the President's son, Elliott Roosevelt (1946 – n.2), chapter 2. For a political eyewitness, see Robert E. Sherwood, *The White House Papers of Harry L. Hopkins*, Eyre & Spottiswoode, London, 1948, vol.1, chapter 16.

8 TNA: FO371/50778; see also CO318/455/2 & 455/4 & 455/6; *The Memoirs of Cordell Hull*, London 1948, vol.2, p.1478. Churchill's speech at the Lord Mayor's Luncheon is available on line: http://www.churchill-society-london.org.uk/EndoBegn.html

9 TNA: CO323/1858 quoting an article in *New York Times*, 18/11/1943; FCB, *International Action and the Colonies*, September 1943, p.19.

10 Lawrence James briefly mentions what would be called 'intelligence' activities by the (British) government of India against American journalists and industrialists in India. (*Raj: The Making and Unmaking of British India*, New York: St. Martin's Press, 1997, p.558)

11 *New York Times*, 20/8/1943; Padmore, 'Anglo-American Plan for Control of Colonies', *Crisis*, #51, November 1944, pp.355-7.

12 Padmore, 'Blue-Print of Post-War Anglo-American Imperialism', *Left*, October 1943, pp.197-202; 'Anglo-American Condominium', *Politics*, May 1944, pp.113-116.

13 LCP *Newsletter*, August 1941, p.136; December 1941; February 1942, p.114. This particular quotation is from TNA: FO371/50807, Churchill to Foreign Secretary, 31/12/1944. *Empire* reported in July 1942 that Churchill's latest statement was that: 'our declared policy in regard to the peoples of the Colonial Empire is in entire harmony with the conceptions underlying the Atlantic Charter'. (p.3) There are some reports in Chapter 6 on how the Atlantic Charter was used by campaigning organisations in the UK.

14 The first meeting was in Trinidad in March 1942. Richard Hart, *Towards Decolonisation*, Kingston: Canoe Press, 1999, p.125. TNA: CO4318/452: CO to Evans, FO, 15/5/1942; CO318/452/BOX; CO318/453; CO318/455/2 & /4 & /6; CO323/1877/4 (9057B) & 877/6 (9086); CO318/455/6, 455/7 & 455/11; FO371/26175; See Charlie Whitham, *Bitter rehearsal: British and American planning for a post-war West Indies*, Westport: Praeger, 2002.

15 Nwafor Orizu, *Africa Speaks*, Nnewi: Horizontal Publishers, 1990, p.94.

16 See Eric Williams, *Inward Hunger: the Education of a Prime Minster*, University of Chicago Press, 1969. At independence in 1962 Williams became Prime Minister of Trinidad and Tobago.

CHAPTER 8

THE UNITED NATIONS ORGANISATION (UNO)

The USA and UK governments, after much discussion between themselves and with other Allies, invited 43 governments to meet in Bretton Woods, USA in April 1944. The main interest of the USA and the UK was to create 'healthy trade conditions to cement a lasting world peace'.[1] This was followed by meetings of representatives of the Soviet Union, Great Britain, the United States and China at Dumbarton Oaks (Washington, D.C.) between August and October 1944. Their principal objective was to discuss the creation of a replacement for the League of Nations and ensure world peace after the end of the war. One primary issue was the membership and constitution of the Security Council and the use of the power of veto in the Council.

African-American historian W.E.B. Du Bois, one of the directors of the National Association for the Advancement of Colored People (NAACP), criticised these discussions in London's *New Leader* on 30 December 1944. He pointed out that the proposals for racial equality made by Japan to the League, and rumoured to have been made by China at Dumbarton Oaks, had not appeared in the published proposals for the formation of the United Nations Organisation (UNO). The proposals permitted the Security Council to limit the rights of the 'Assembly'. The Council would consist of 6 representatives of the 'great powers', who would thus control the whole UNO. Colonial people would only be represented by 'their masters'. Du Bois was adamant that 'to set up an international order with nearly half mankind disfranchised and socially enslaved is to court disaster'.

The Indian Delegation at Bretton Woods, 1944

Fifty-one countries were represented at the initial meetings in San Francisco in February 1945. However, the agenda was set and controlled by the major powers. The NAACP served as 'official consultants' on racial and colonial issues to the American delegation. According to one report, they met with an 'indifferent and sometimes an antagonistic delegation'. The issue of the colonies' independence was omitted from the agreed Charter. The Bill of Rights 'omitted mention of colonised people'. Their inclusion had been supported by China and the USSR, but was blocked by the UK and the USA.[2]

A **Trusteeship Council** was set up for the 'administration and supervision of such territories as may be placed thereunder by subsequent individual agreements'. The trustees would have to 'ensure equal treatment in social, economic and commercial matters for all Members of the United Nations'. This was to apply to 'territories which may be detached from enemy states as a result of the Second World War'. Agreement had to be reached as to which territories were to come under Trusteeship Council. Colonies 'belonging' to members of the UN were excluded by Article 78:

> The trusteeship system shall not apply to territories which have Members of the United Nations. Relationship among which shall be based on respect for the principle of sovereign equality.[3]

What 'sovereign equality' meant was not defined.

The Charter was signed in June 1945. As Padmore noted,

> Although India was 'represented' at the San Francisco Conference by a few hand-picked Indian members of the Viceroy's cabinet, the subject peoples of the Colonial Empire were not allowed to send unofficial observers to the conference although one of the main questions discussed concerned the future status of these dependent territories.[4]

— — —

NOTES

1   Sigrid Arne, *United Nations Primer*, New York: Farrar & Rinehart, 1945, p.72.
2   From Marika Sherwood, '"There Is No New Deal for the blackman in San Francisco": African Attempts to Influence the Founding Conference of the Unites Nations, April – July 1945', *Int. Jnl. of African Historical Studies*, 29/1, 1996, pp.71-94; the final quotation is from Du Bois, head of the NAACP consultants, p.90. See also Marika Sherwood, 'The United Nations: Caribbean and African-American Attempts to Influence the Founding Conference in San Francisco in 1945', *Jnl. of Caribbean History*, 29/1, 1995, pp.27-58.
3   Arne (1945 – n.1), p.143. For criticisms of Trusteeship, see Padmore, 'Trusteeship – the New Imperialism', *New Leader*, 2, 9 & 16 February, 1946.
4   Padmore, 'British Refused African Conference Representation', *Pittsburgh Courier*, 16/6/1945, p.12.

SECTION 5

THE IMMEDIATE POST-WAR YEARS
JUNE 1945 – JUNE 1948

On 30 April 1945 Hitler committed suicide and on 8 May 1945 the Allies formally accepted the unconditional surrender of the armed forces of Nazi Germany. The war against Japan ended when the US dropped atomic bombs on Hiroshima and Nagasaki on August 6 and 9. About a quarter of a million people were killed.

As **Britain** was no longer at war in Europe, 'colonial' protesters no longer had to fear imprisonment if they criticised the colonial powers. One important conference followed another, demanding equality and independence.

In the UK the Conservatives lost the July 1945 national elections, but the Labour Party did not want to deviate from the established policy towards Britain's empire. This was emphasised by Herbert Morrison, Deputy Prime Minister and Leader of the House of Commons, on his visit to Canada and the USA early in 1946. When asked if the Labour Government 'will preside over the liquidation of the British empire', he replied 'No fear! We are great friends of the jolly old Empire and are going to stick to it.' Just how important the colonies were to Britain was emphasised by the Minister for Economic Affairs late in 1947:

> the whole future of the sterling group and its ability to survive [relies on] a quick and vast development of colonial resources... The production of food and raw materials in the colonies for the United Kingdom [is essential] so we won't have to buy for US dollars.[1]

The crucial **importance of the African colonies** is also manifested by the amount they earned for Britain from exports. For example, the Gold Coast earned $100 million in 1946 from the export of cocoa, gold and industrial diamonds. In 1947 the Minister of Economic Affairs told the African Governors Conference in London that 'the whole future of the sterling group and its ability to survive' depended on the colonies.[2]

The sterling assets of the colonies in London at the end of 1946 were £800 million, of which £115 million was West Africa's. So there should have been no problems with financing 'development'.[3] But if this article, headed 'Black Ingratitude' in *Reynolds News* of 8 September 1946 reflected general attitudes, it is no wonder that little was done:

These blacks must realise that if their labour wasn't cheap they couldn't have the privilege of engaging in civilised industry at all... as Winston Churchill said 'if we raised native labour to the same standards as our own, what would happen to our foreign investments?'

All over the world the coloured races are forgetting their place.

A **Peace Conference** was held in Paris in the summer of 1946, to attempt to decide the fate of colonies taken from Italy and those under the mandates systems imposed by the League of Nations after WWI. The UN had decided to set up a Trusteeship Council to deal with the issue, but there was much disagreement about its role and powers. General Smuts of South Africa was one of those causing difficulties by demanding the incorporation of South-Western Africa into South Africa.[4]

When the **Trusteeship Council** was eventually established, its vice-chair was Sir Alan Burns, the just-retired governor of the Gold Coast. Burns is reported as stating at a luncheon for the Foreign Missions Conference in New York that

the major problems obstructing general improvement in Africa are the fear of the supernatural and an inferiority complex. Africans tend to blame others for much they could do or undo themselves, that is, they refuse to admit their own faults... The future of Africa is bright, but a small group of not too well educated persons are clamouring for self-government which will confuse the issue and set the clock back.[5]

In 1946 the Colonial Office prepared a **'Memorandum on Legislation Involving Colour Discrimination'** in Africa, Borneo and Malaya. The West Indies is absent except regarding 'master and servant', ie, employment laws. On the islands, and in the East African colonies, legislation made 'breaching a contract by a servant a criminal offense'. What needed to be done regarding the gross discriminations became the subject of much discussion.

Sir Alan Burns, 24-November-1947

In May 1947 the three major colonial powers, **France, Belgium and Britain**, met in Paris to attempt to agree on a new policy towards colonies and to co-operate on some issues, such as medical and veterinary services. The agreement was to meet again.[6]

The issue of racial discrimination throughout Europe's West African colonies was raised at the **World Federation of Trade Unions** meeting on 15 June 1947. The British representatives refused to agree to suggestions for improved medical services for workers or social security legislation in the colonies.[7]

The next two chapters will outline *some* of the political struggles in Africa, India and the West Indies, and then in Britain after end of the war until mid-1948.

Vientam's leader, Ho Chi Minh, at
the Paris Peace Conference, 1946

NOTES

1   *The Times*, 12/1/1946, p.3; *New York Times*, 13/11/1947, p.4.
2   *New York Herald Tribune*, 16/12/1947, p.34; *New York Times*, 13/11/1947, p.4.
3   *Colonial Review*, September 1947.
4   GP, 'Britain Acts To Bury Issue of Colonies, *Chicago Defender*, 10/8/1946, p.1; see also his articles in *West African Pilot*, 28, 30, 31 August & 2, 3, 4 September 1946.
5   *Chicago Defender*, 9/2/1946, p.7; 23/2/1946, p.4; 10/8/1946, p.1; 26/10/1946, p.1; *New York Times*, 16/12/1947, p.23.
6   *The Times*, 21/5/1947, p.3; 24/5, p.5 & 14/11/1947, p.5.
7   *The Times*, 16/6/1947, p.3.

CHAPTER 9

THE EMPIRE

WEST AND EAST AFRICA

Conditions were dire. The **price of imported foods** and other goods had increased grossly. Unemployment was rife. For example, in 1946, 60% of discharged servicemen registered for paid employment. The highest proportion to be offered work was in Sierra Leone, where 45% of the 7,922 registered (out of the total number then discharged, 15,899) had been offered work.[1]

The ongoing level of exploitation by colonial policies is demonstrated, for example, by comparing the amount of tax paid to the UK and to the Gold Coast by British companies operating there. In 1946 they paid £990,645 to the UK and £498,834 to the Gold Coast administration.[2]

In 1946 **West Africans troops in India and Burma** were still awaiting repatriation. Their living conditions were so dreadful that the LCP in London protested. In 1947 the issue was also raised in Parliament.[3] But some learned their politics there. Waruhiu Itote, a literate Kenyan villager, could not have been the only African soldier who learned about the necessity to struggle for independence. While stationed in India he met a 'powerful Negro from the American South'. Stephenson, the 'Negro', told the Africans clustered around him much about the situation for 'Negroes' in the USA, and said 'The whites who are fighting now will be heroes in their own countries forever and amen, while you Africans will be heroes for a day and then you'll be forgotten. If you want to be heroes, why don't you fight for your own countries?' Itote then

Corporal Waruhiu Itote, KAR, arrested in 1954 for membership of the "Mau Mau"

relates a conversation with an Indian, who said to him: 'While you are here in India, you ought to pay attention to what we are doing... We Indians are fighting for others in this war, but in return we've received a promise of Independence when it ends. I have seen many Africans fighting alongside our men, but I haven't heard what demands you've made for the end of the war.' 'Conversations like this', Itote says, continued throughout his stay in India.[4]

Up to 200,000 workers went on strike in **Nigeria** in June 1945 as the government refused to raise wages to keep pace with the rise in prices. Nationalist Nnamdi Azikiwe had formed the National Council of Nigeria and the Cameroons (NCNC) in 1944. His two newspapers, the *West African Pilot* and the *Daily Comet*, which supported the strike, were banned. The West African Students Union and the International African Service Bureau in the UK raised £225 to support the strikers.[5] In 1947, according to official figures, 43,533 ex-soldiers were still unemployed.[6] Colour discrimination was highlighted when Colonial Office official Ivor Cummings was refused his government-booked accommodation at Lagos's Bristol Hotel in 1947, as he was not White. As soon as this became known, the hotel was attacked. At the ensuing mass meeting, it was demanded that colour discrimination should be made illegal and all racial segregation should be banned.[7]

In August 1947 the **National Council of Nigeria and Cameroons** sent a deputation to Britain to attempt to cajole the government into revising the imposed constitution and move towards independence. They were unsuccessful. At the mass meeting on their return, some advocated violence while others recommended approaching the United Nations. 'We are not anti-white or anti-British', Azikiwe said, 'but after fighting in the war for democracy we are determined to win a democracy.'[8]

On the Gold Coast the **United Gold Coast Convention** (UGCC) was formed on 5 August 1947, to attempt to cohere peoples for the fight for independence. Troubles were looming in the colony as prices of all imported goods had increased hugely. The numbers unemployed rose with the closure of the military bases. The ex-servicemen were dissatisfied with their pensions, and workers with their wages. For example, gold miners were out on strike in October 1947.[9] In early 1948 a boycott was organised of all shops selling imported goods at grossly inflated prices. When ex-servicemen marched to deliver a petition to the Governor, charging that they had deviated from the permitted route, the police fired at them. Three ex-soldiers were killed and many wounded. *West Africa* reported on 13 March that throughout the colony 21 had been killed and 228 wounded. Accusing them of fomenting the march if not the ensuing riots, the UGCC leaders were imprisoned.

Though **new constitutions in the Gold Coast and Nigeria** gave Africans some representation on the Legislative Assemblies, there was much criticism. The proposals for **East Africa** also permitted both African and Indian representatives; but the 20,000 White settlers in Kenya would have 11 elected representatives and the 70,000 Indians five, while the (roughly) 4 million

Africans would have four members nominated by the Governor. There was also a proposal for an Inter-Territorial Council and Assembly for Kenyans, Tanganyikans and Ugandans, with similar representation. The White settlers objected – and won the support of the Labour Party. In April 1947 the **Kenya African Union** joined forces with the local East African National Congress to form the **African-Asiatic United Front Committee** to fight for 'equal citizenship rights'.[10]

INDIA

It was to be expected that disturbances should escalate, almost from day to day throughout 1946: strikes proliferated; the Royal Indian Navy mutinied in Bombay (now Mumbai) and British troops were called in to restore 'peace'. They killed 223 demonstrators and 9 sailors. Servicemen, disgruntled at the slow pace of demobilization were also protesting.[11] Conflicts between Muslims and Hindus escalated: thousands killed each other and more were killed and wounded by the peace-keeping troops.

The British Government gave up hope of retaining India within the Empire. Admiral Mountbatten, appointed as the new Viceroy/Governor- General, was sent out in March 1947 to mediate. The negotiations resulted in the partitioning of 'British India' into India and Pakistan. The British Parliament passed the Indian Independence Act. On 14 August 1947 **Pakistan was declared a separate nation** with Muhammad Ali Jinnah as the Governor-General. The following day **India became independent**; Pandit Jawaharlal Nehru was appointed Prime Minister. Violent clashes between Hindus, Sikhs and Muslims followed.

WEST INDIES

Strikes continued throughout the islands. For example, five demonstrators were killed during the strike of the railwaymen in **Jamaica**. (All railway workers had to work a 54-hour week and often 12-hour days. Overtime pay was only for those working longer than a 14-hour shift.)[12] This led to more street fighting, and more protests. The Governor responded by forbidding street meetings and demonstrations. Fifteen patients were burned to death in a 'mental asylum' set on fire during a demonstration.[13] The unemployment situation was made worse by the return of thousands of war-time workers from the USA. The Colonial Office estimated that there were 50,000 'unemployed or underemployed' in Jamaica in 1948.[14]

Strikes also proliferated in **Trinidad**, some instigated by trade union leader Uriah Butler, recently released from prison. The Government discussed sending additional troops to the islands to maintain the peace. There was special concern about Trinidad by the Chiefs of Staff, who feared that the 'unrest... might lead to intervention by personnel of the US bases which would gravely injure our prestige'.[15]

There was much discontent with the Legislative Council, half of whose members were elected and half nominated by the Governor. The Governor had the deciding vote. A Constitutional Reform Committee was set up and drew up a new Constitution. Eric Williams, the historian and future prime minister, described it as 'the almost unbelievable fiasco of the first Ministerial system under the 1950 Constitution'.[16]

Uriah Butler arrived in the UK on 9 September, to press for Home Rule for Trinidad. The Secretary of State for the Colonies refused to see him, but the Colonial Office did offer an appointment.[17]

Universal suffrage was granted to all the 'British' islands by 1954.

— — —

NOTES

1 *West Africa*, 14/12/1946, p. 1166.

2 NARA: RG59, Box 6211, file 848N4212, Report on the Gold Coast.

3 *The Times*, 16/3/1946, p.2.

4 Waruhiu Itote (General China), *Mau Mau General*, Nairobi: East African Publishing House, 1967, pp.11-15. Itote went on to fight with the Land and Freedom Army (the 'Mau Mau') for Kenya's independence. He was captured and imprisoned 1954-1962. After independence (December 1963) he served in the Kenya Youth Service.

5 Wogu Ananaba, *The Trade Union Movement in Nigeria*, London: C. Hurst, 1969, p.58.

6 G.O. Olusanya, 'The Role of Ex-Servicemen in Nigerian Politics', *Jnl. of Modern African Studies*, 6/2, 1968, p.227.

7 John Flint, 'Scandal at the Bristol Hotel: Some thoughts on racial discrimination in Britain 1939–47', *Jnl. of Imperial and Commonwealth History*, 12/1, 1983, pp.74-93. The Governor refused to tender an apology, but promised to eliminate segregation and 'colour discrimination'.

8 *Daily Worker*, 9/9/1947, p.3.

9 *The Times*, 1/10/1947, p.8.

10 *Socialist Leader*, 24/5/1947, p.1. *Hansard*, 28/1/1947, vol.432, col.170.

11 Lawrence James, *Raj: The Making and Unmaking of British India*, New York: St. Martin's Press, 1997, pp.592-598.

12 Padmore, 'Facts Behind Jamaica Labour Riots', *New Leader*, 2/3/1946, p.4.

13 *New Leader*, 2/3/1946, p.4; *Times*, 12/4/1946, p.4.

14 TNA: CO537/2583, internal memo 15/6/1948.

15 *Times*, 24/1/1947, p.3. TNA: CAB122/1052 (file 12/5), Chief of Staffs Committee – Caribbean Area, 20 April 1948 (JP[48]42[final]).

16 Eric Williams, *History of the People of Trinidad and Tobago*, Port-of-Spain: PNM Publishing, 1962, p.243.

17 TNA: CO537/4220, file 96803/1.

CHAPTER 10

CONFERENCES AND PROTESTS IN BRITAIN

1945

'Long live the international bond between the white and black workers', is how Jomo Kenyatta, I.T.A. Wallace-Johnson, Dr Peter Milliard, T.R. Makonnen and George Padmore concluded their letter printed in the centre of the first page of the *New Leader* of 5 May 1945. They, and the others reported on that page, were celebrating May Day, traditionally the International Workers' Day, or Labour Day. In some colonies it was used for broader purposes: for example, at the huge May Day celebration of the TUC in Lagos a resolution demanded full adult suffrage for the people of Nigeria.

The long war was almost over. Hitler was declared dead. Kenyatta and his colleagues wanted to do what they could to ensure that 'peace' would also bring freedom and equality. In their letter they had argued that:

Anglo-Nigerian Co-operation

You are invited to a

Public Meeting

on TUESDAY 9th SEPTEMBER

at 7-30 p.m.

in

HOULDSWORTH HALL

Deansgate

HOW CAN NIGERIA HELP BRITAIN ?

THE SPEAKERS

Goodwill Mission of the National Council of Nigeria and Cameroons now visiting this country will include:

Dr. Nnamdi Azikiwe, M.L.C.
Prince Adeleke Adedoyin, M.L.C.
Cheif Nyong-Essien, M.L.C.
Dr. Olorun-Nimbe, M.L.C.
Mrs. F. Ransome-Kuti
Mr. Paul M. Kale
Mallam Bukar Ditcharima

Auspices:
THE PAN-AFRICAN FEDERATION, 58 Oxford Road
Manchester, I.

W. H. Gorman & Son, Richmond Street, M/c. 1

For at this moment of rejoicing we must never forget that there are still hundreds of millions in Asia, Africa, and other subject lands, living under Fascist-like conditions, and that there can be no lasting peace and security for Europe and America while the ruling classes of these Continents continue to enslave the darker peoples of the world... It is the bounden duty and moral obligation of all who subscribe to human progress to support the struggles of the Colonial peoples for the right to Self-Determination.

In February Padmore and his colleagues in the **Pan-African Federation** had seized the opportunity presented by the presence of some colonial delegates at the World Federation of Trade Unions

Conference (WFTU) in Paris. They invited them to visit Manchester to discuss how to move forward on the 'self-determination' issue. The Manifesto passed called on the forthcoming UNO founding conference to establish policies for securing equal rights, economic and educational development and full self-government 'within definite time-limits'. An agreement was reached to hold two different conferences: one was the Subject People's Conference, and the other the Pan-African Conference, held in Manchester in October 1945.[1]

In the letter sent to the Prime Minister the delegates argued that 'imperialism is one of the major causes of war'; if 'the domination of peoples does not cease', new wars were inevitable.[2] According to Peter Abrahams' article 'The Congress in Perspective', the aim of the Subject People's Conference was 'the setting up of some permanent organisation for the co-ordination of the Colonial struggle'.[3]

The urgency of holding a conference and of bringing together all colonised peoples, was emphasised by the interest of the USA in the colonies, and the forthcoming establishment of the United Nations. As outlined in the journal *East Africa and Rhodesia*, which was the voice of the colonizers,

> Extremists in the United States and Great Britain look to San Francisco to introduce internationalization of dependent areas.... Could His Majesty's Government be willing to agree under pressure to some accommodation acceptable to Washington? The Prime Minister had said that 'matters affecting the British colonial territories will not be discussed at San Francisco'.

The importance of the United Nations had been well recognised by the political activists. The many Black organisations attending the AGM of the **League of Coloured Peoples** in March agreed a *Manifesto on Africa in the Post-War World for presentation to the United Nations Conference, San Francisco, April 1945*. This was a replication of the Manifesto agreed in February. The LCP sent copies to Black organisations around the world and to the Prime Minister, Secretaries of State and the British representative in San Francisco. The government decided all it had to do was send an acknowledgement of receipt of the letter. At about the same time the **Federation of Indian Associations** in Britain distributed a similar Memorandum, asking for the release of all political prisoners, and for freedom. All the Federation's letters with their Memorandum were returned to them by the censor.[4]

The next major conference was organised by the International African Service Bureau and its many contacts. The **All-Colonial Peoples' Conference** (sometimes called the Subject Peoples' Conference) was held in London on 10 June. There were 40 delegates with full voting rights and 25 'unofficial observers', representing 'subject peoples' around the world. The resolutions asked for independence and the ending of all racial discrimination. It was also decided to set up a permanent committee to fight for these aims. There was a follow-up conference on 10 October, focussing on the re-imposition of imperialism in South-East Asia. The resolutions passed demanded freedom for Indo-China, the Dutch East Indies, India, Burma and Ceylon.[5]

In July a rally was organised by the major Black organisations to **support the Nigerian strikers**' demands and for the removal of the order banning the local newspapers. Financial support was sought for the strikers. Support meetings were held around the country.[6]

After a number of consultative meetings, the Pan-African Federation organised **a Pan-African Congress** in Manchester in October 1945. The resolutions passed included demands for the
- complete and absolute independence for the peoples of West Africa;
- 'democratic rights and self-government' for the East African colonies;
- self-government and federation in the West Indies;
- in Britain, 'discrimination on account of race, creed or colour be made a criminal offence by law'.

A Memorandum to the United Nations, demanding full representation was agreed. W.E.B. Du Bois, who had chaired some of the sessions was asked

Pan-African Congress in Manchester in October 1945

to circulate it to organisations in the USA and then present it to the UNO. The 'Declaration to the Colonial People' stressed the importance of forming a united front in the struggle against colonialism. Among those attending the Congress who soon returned home to begin or to continue struggles for independence, were Wallace-Johnson (Sierra Leone); Obafemi Awolowo, Jaja Wachuku and H.O Davies (Nigeria); Ashie-Nikoi, Joe Appiah and Kwame Nkrumah (Gold Coast); Garba-Jahumpa (Gambia); Jomo Kenyatta (Kenya) and Ken Hill (Jamaica) .

1946

In January the **India League** organised a demonstration in Trafalgar Square, calling for the independence of India and immediate election for a constituent assembly. British intervention in Indonesia was condemned. The demonstrators marched to the Foreign Office and the India Office to hand in the resolutions.[7]

The **British Centre Against Imperialism** was re-launched at a conference on 23-24 February. White MPs chaired most of the sessions. The main speakers were Professor Gangulee, who spoke on India and the Far East; George Padmore and Frank Horrabin talked about African and the West Indian issues; Fenner Brockway spoke on the struggle against imperialism. The main decision was that 'action to end imperialism must come quickly'.[8]

Hansard HC Deb 27 February 1946 vol 419 c392W
AFRICAN TROOPS (WHIPPING)
Mr. Sorensen asked the Secretary of State for the Colonies whether the suspension of the penalty of whipping for delinquent West African soldiers is preparatory to the total abolition or drastic restriction of this form of punishment
Mr. Creech Jones I am not clear what my hon. Friend means by the reference to the suspension of the penalty of whipping. Reports from the Military Commanders in East and West Africa on the matter have recently been received and are being considered in consultation with my right hon. Friend the Secretary of State for War.

I.T.A. Wallace-Johnson, Kwame Nkrumah and a White colleague, Betty Dorman, planned a new organisation, the **West African National Secretariat** (WANS). They toured the UK to contact interested organisations. WANS' aims were to support the economic, social and political struggles of colonial peoples. It issued a Manifesto, which was widely distributed. In September WANS announced that it was going to form a 'National Congress along the lines of the Indian Congress.... (with) the ultimate aim of United Socialist States of Africa'. In March the first issue of WANS' journal *The New African*, appeared with the motto 'For Unity and Absolute Independence'.[9]

On 1 February 1946 WANS held a conference. The resolutions stated that the United Nations should help 'West Africans achieve independence now'; and called upon the UN 'to take such steps as will bring about the complete liquidation of the colonial system'. To follow up, WANS and WASU held a 3-day conference in August-September, on the theme of 'Unity and Independence of all West Africa'. Under the leadership of Nkrumah WANS worked closely with other organisations and with Fenner Brockway.

Racial Pride and Prejudice by Sri Lankan-born Eric J. Dingwall was published with a chapter on 'The colour bar in Great Britain'. He reported on many instances of the 'colour bar' and argued that children in Britain were taught that the 'non-white population of the world is…inferior…destined to remain subject to the economic and social domination of those who had vanquished them… [children should be taught] how the possession of white skin is in no way a guarantee of social or political dominance.' (pp. 114, 122)

The LCP complained to the Secretary of State for War about the 'bad conditions' in which RWAFF men were living in the 'Far East' while awaiting repatriation.[10]

MASS DEMONSTRATION OF COLONIAL AND SUBJECT PEOPLES

in TRAFALGAR SQUARE, London,

On SUNDAY, DECEMBER 9th, at 2 p.m.

Speakers from Africa, West Indies, Java, Indo-China and other Colonial Areas.

"THE COLOUR BAR IN GT. BRITAIN AND THE COLONIES."

Sponsored by the Pan-African Federation, 58, Oxford Road, Manchester.

New Leader, 1/12/1945, p.3

1947

The 'termination of British rule in West Africa' was the main demand at the 'Extraordinary General Conference' organised by **WASU** on 13 April. The Resolution would be sent to the British and colonial governments, and distributed as widely as possible to the 'peoples of West Africa'.[11]

Nnamdi Azikiwe led a delegation from the **National Council of Nigeria and Cameroons (NCNC)**, to New York and London. Extraordinarily for those years, the delegates included a woman, Funmilayo Ransome-Kuti. They argued that as independence had been granted to India, it should be granted to Africans. If the Colonial Office refused, they would appeal to the United Nations. The delegates also proposed that 'sources of raw materials in Africa should be open to all'. Under the present 'Protectionist' system Africans did not benefit. For example, though Nigeria and the Gold Coast produced two-thirds of the world's cocoa, the farmers had to sell to the British Cocoa Marketing

AFRICAN GOOD-WILL MISSION TO BRITAIN

The British People & all Friends of Africa

ARE INVITED TO

Russel Square thence to Trafalgar Square

on Sunday, September 14th, 1947, at 3 p.m.

TO JOIN

A DEMONSTRATION
BY NIGERIANS

In support of the Nigerian Delegation's demand for a more Democratic Constitution and for immediate steps to be taken now towards Self-Government for Nigeria and the British Cameroons

SPEAKERS MAY INCLUDE

Dr. Nnamdi Azikiwe (President, N.C.N.C., Elected Member of the Legislative Council of Nigeria)

Mr. George Padmore (W. Indies)   Mallam Aminu Kano (Nigeria)
Mr. Nkrumah (Gold Coast)   Mr. Usmani (India)
Mr. Makonnen (East Africa)   Mr. Murugiah (Malaya)
Mr. Sam Morris (W. Indies)   Mr. Mohamed Ali (Indonesia)
Mr. Peter Abraham (South Africa)   Mr. Bakare (Nigeria)
Miss Otubisin (Nigeria)
Mr. Ojiako (Secretary, Nigeria Union of Great Britain and Ireland)

ORGANISATIONS INVITED : West African Students' Union, West Indian Students' Union, Indian Students' Union, League of Coloured Peoples, The Pan-African Federation, West African National Secretariat, Coloured Workers' Association, British Centre for Colonial Freedom, Gold Coast Students' Union, Over-seas League, Sierra-Leone Union

Universal Publicity Service, 74 George Street, Croydon (CROydon 0338)

Board, which controlled the prices. The Secretary of State for Colonies refused to change the new constitution recently imposed on Nigeria, or entertain ideas of independence.[12]

About 1,000 people attended the rally in Trafalgar Square on 14 September in support of the 'demand for a more Democratic Constitution and for immediate steps to be taken now towards Self-Government for Nigeria and the British Cameroons'. Among the speakers were Nnamdi Azikiwe, representatives of WANS, of the British Centre for Colonial Freedom, of the Nigerian Union of Great Britain and of the Indian Students' Union, as well as the editor of the journal *Pan-Africa*, and a law student from Malaya.[13]

WANS convened a meeting on 21 November, where resolutions were passed for complete independence, following the Atlantic Charter principles.[14]

Ernest Marke

Ernest Marke an ex-seaman from Sierra Leone who had been involved in many of the past years' political activities was one of the founders of the **Coloured Workers Association** (CWA) in 1945 The *West African Pilot (*19/12/1947, pp.1, 3) reported the CWA's first annual general meeting, held at an unknown date. Among the speakers was Kwame Nkrumah, who had been involved in recruiting members. Both he and Fenner Brockway of the British Centre for Colonial Freedom 'stressed that there should be freedom for all peoples in England and other coloured peoples of the world'.[15]

A New World

The new states of **Pakistan,** under the leadership of Jinnah, and **India** under the leadership of Nehru, celebrated their independence on 14 and 15 August 1947.[16] Mohandas Gandhi lived to see independence: he died on 30 January 1948.

Nkrumah returned to the **Gold Coast** as the Secretary of the new political party, the United Gold Coast Convention. He was among those imprisoned for supposedly fomenting the riots of 1948 in Accra.[17] He resigned from the UGCC, set up the Convention People's Party and began the struggle for independence and African Unity.

The USA replaced its war-time 'Lend Lease' scheme with the Marshall Plan, which aimed to prevent the spread of communism across Europe and its colonies. In return for this new loan, Britain permitted the USA access to all the raw materials in its African colonies and to market US products there.[18] The Plan 'secured America's economic influence over Europe', split the world between 'communism' and 'democracy', led to the Cold and other wars for domination.[19]

Both the UK and the USA condemned nationalist struggles as communist.

The **Empire Windrush** arrived at Tilbury, London docks, on 22 June 1948, carrying 493 passengers, mainly from Jamaica.[20] Most of them were young men, many discharged ex-servicemen who had hoped to find work at home. But there were no jobs in Jamaica; and they were pretty sure that there would be work in the UK. So they paid their passage (often with borrowed money), intending to earn enough in the UK to be able to return home and set up workshops, businesses. But that is not how it worked out......

The first major post-war riots against Black peoples took place in Liverpool in August 1948.

Notes

1   'Pan-African Conference set for Paris in Fall', *Chicago Defender*, 10/3/1945 & 'Call for Pan-African Parley', 17/3/1945; 'Pan-African Congress Plans Paris Meeting', *Pittsburgh Courier*, 3/3/1945. See Hakim Adi and Marika Sherwood, *The 1945 Manchester Pan-African Congress Revisited*, London: New Beacon Books, 1995; Marika Sherwood, *Manchester and the 1945 Pan-African Congress*, London: Savannah Press, 1995.

2   'Big Struggle Begins for African Freedom', *New Leader*, 20/10/1945.

3   'Colonial and Coloured Unity', reproduced in Adi & Sherwood (1995 - n.1). The plans for setting up an organisation were also published in the *West African Pilot*, 30/5/1945, *Chicago Defender*, 17/3/1945, *Karachi Dawn*, 17/3/1945.

4   LCP *Newsletter*, April 1945, p.14; copy of Manifesto in W.E.B. Du Bois Papers, reel 57, frames 0534-6. Marika Sherwood, '"Diplomatic Platitudes": The Atlantic Charter, the United National and Colonial Independence', *Immigrants & Minorities*, 15/2, July 1996, pp.135-150.

5   These Subject Peoples' Conferences have not yet been documented.

6   Hakim Adi, *West Africans in Britain 1900 – 1960*, London: Lawrence & Wishart, 1998. p.125; Adi & Sherwood (1995 – n.1), pp.21-2.

7   *The Times*, 28/1/1945, p.2.

8   *New Leader*, 16/2 & 2/3/1946; *Socialist Leader*, 2/2 & 2/3/1946. There is a full report by Padmore in the *New Leader*, 2/3/1946, p.3 & 9/3/1946, p.6. Brockway

and Horrabin were old members of the India League (under Krishna Menon's leadership since the early 1930s), which had been campaigning for independence for India. Sadly Brockway barely mentions the Centre in his autobiography, *Towards Tomorrow*, London: Hart-Davis, 1977, p.152.

9   For reports in Nigeria on WANS' formation, see *West African Pilot*, 19/2/1946, p.2, 20/2/1946, (editorial); *Comet* 11/9/1946, p.1; Quotation from *New Leader*, 21/9/1946, p.2. On Nkrumah's years abroad, see Marika Sherwood, *Kwame Nkrumah: the Years Abroad 1935-1947*, Freedom Publications, Ghana, 1996.

10   *The Times*, 16/3/1946, p.2.

11   *West African Pilot*, 24/4/1947, pp.1, 4.

12   Three are copious reports in *West African Pilot*, Zik's paper. On visit to USA, see eg *Afro-American*, 21/6/1947, p.7. *The Times* (14/8/1947, p.3) noted that the delegation was received by the Secretary of State for the Colonies. That Mrs Ransome- Kuti was part of the delegation is in Padmore's report in *Chicago Defender*, 23/8/1947, p.15.

13   *Anglo-American*, 21/6/1947, p.7; *Daily Worker*, 4/7/1947; *The Times*, 14/8/1947, p.3; *Manchester Guardian*, 10/9/1947, p.6; *Chicago Defender*, 27/9/1947, p.15; *West African Pilot*, 20/101947, pp.1, 2, 3; TNA: CO583/292/30658, flyer for the Trafalgar Square meeting.

14   *Socialist Leader*, 6/12/1947, p.6; *Ashanti Pioneer*, 29/12/1947, p. 1.

15   *West African Pilot*, 19/12/1947, pp.1, 3. I knew Mr Marke and have some brief notes of my conversations with him. Nkrumah mentions his work for the CWA in his *Autobiography*, Edinburgh: Thomas Nelson & Sons, 1957, pp.58-9. There are no adequate histories of the work of the CWA.

16   There is a very useful summary of the independence discussions in K.C. Arora, *Indian Nationalist Movement in Britain (1930 – 1949)*, New Delhi: M C Mittal, 1992, pp.133-136.

17   See, eg 'The Grievances Behind the Riots', *African World*, April 1948, pp.11-12; in his article in the *West African Pilot* (20/3/1948) Padmore emphasises how much exports from its African colonies earns Britain, then heavily indebted to the USA. See also his article, 'Unrest in the Gold Coast' in *Socialist Commentary*, #7, April 1948, pp.159-160.

18   Padmore, 'World Views', *Chicago Defender*, 15/5/1948, p.15; Brigadier G.S. Brunskill, 'Bastion for Democracy', *Christian Science Monitor*, 15/5/1948, p.WM2.

19   See Charles L. Mee, *The Marshall Plan*, New York: Simon & Schuster, 1984. See *African Affairs* (#197, October 1950, pp.302-308) for the transcript of the address by Abbot Low Moffat, one of the administrators of the Marshall Plan at the US Embassy in London to the Royal African Society in July 1950. He describes in detail the already existing US involvements with Africa.

20   The Secretary of State for the Colonies advised the Cabinet that the Jamaican governor had been asked to 'ascertain the ringleaders of the enterprise' and that 'every possible step has been taken by the Colonial Office and by the Jamaican Government to discourage these influxes'. (TNA: CO537/2583)

Index

(footnotes are not listed)

A

Abrahams, Peter 107, 111
Abyssinia (Ethiopia) 14, 24, 33
Adams, David, MP 62
Advani, Arjan Baharsing 72
'Africa and the Post-War World'
  Manifesto 83, 84
Africa and the World, banned 8, 19
Africa, imports from 49-50
  - export earnings 98
African-Americans 41, 73-74, 76
African-Asiatic United Front
  Committee 103
African Governors Conference 98
African Medical Officer, salary 60, 77
African National Congress (ANC) 9
African Sentinel 9
Africans in Britain, early history 2
Air Raid Precaution Service (ARP) 16,
  72
Alcindor, Cyril Charles 25
Aldred, Guy 17
Ali, Mohamed 111
All-Colonial Peoples' (Subject
  Peoples') Conference 107
All-India Trade Union Congress 20
Anglo-American Caribbean
  Commission (AACP) 93
Annan, J.S. 84
Anthony, Seth 35
Antigua 41
Anti-Imperialist Congress 17
Anti-Slavery and Aborigines Protection
  Society 79
Appiah, Joe 109
Aruba 36
Ashie-Nikoi 109
Atlantic Charter 60, 67, 80, 81, 82, 83,
  88, 89-92, 112

'Atlantic Charter and British West
  Africa' Memorandum 82
Atomic bombs 24, 98
Atta, W. Ofori 20
Attlee, Clement 91
Australia 1, 10, 26, 32, 36
Australian Aborigines 2, 26
Auxiliary Fire Service (UK) 72
Auxiliary Territorial Service (ATS),
  UK 37; from the West Indies 71, 76
Awolowo, Obafemi 109
Axis powers 24, 58, 88; surrender 83
Azikiwe, Nnamdi 63, 82, 102, 106,
  110, 111, 112

B

Bader, Lilian 25
Bahamas 41
Bakare, Mr. 111
Bankole, T.A. 84
Bankole-Bright, Hubert 14
Barbados 6, 50, 65, 66
Barber, Captain D.H. 31, 71
Basuto / Basutoland 9, 32, 34
Bechuanaland 9
Belgium, 50, 99
Bell, Gerald 24, 26
Bengal, famine 60, 82
Bhandari, Dr. 58
Birmingham 76
Blackman, Peter 20
'Black' Britons in the military 25, 77
Bombay (Mumbai) 32, 39, 103
Bomber Command 37
Borneo 99
Bourne, Stephen 25
Braithwaite, Chris 14
Bristol Hotel, Lagos 102
British Centre Against Imperialism /
  for Colonial Freedom 19, 109, 111,
  112
British Empire 1
British Empire Exhibition 17-18
British Guiana (Guyana) 6, 41, 50, 67

British Honduras (Belize) Forestry Unit in Scotland 53-4
Brockway, Fenner 19, 109, 110, 112
Buganda, Resident 30
Burma 19, 32, 33, 34, 35, 36, 38, 39, 41, 60, 78, 101, 108
Burns, Sir Alan 63, 99
Bustamente, Alexander 6, 66
Bustamente Industrial Trade Union 66
Butler, Uriah 6, 7, 65, 103, 104

C

'Call to All Peoples' Manifesto 83
Cameroons 24
Canada 1, 26, 32
Canada, West Indian immigrants 26, 36
Canadian Air Force 24, 26
Canadian Expeditionary Force 26
Cape Corps 35
Cardiff 5, 25, 52, 71, 76
Caribbean Regiment 30, 37, 38
Caribbean Sea, U-boats in 36
'Casualty' rates, colonial 32-3, 38, 41
Censorship in Britain / colonies 58, 59, 79
Ceylon 3, 19, 108
'Charter for Colonial Freedom' 81
'Charter for Coloured Peoples' 82-83
China 24, 96, 97
Churchill, Winston 41, 59, 60, 74, 80, 88-92
'Civil Liberty in the Colonial Empire' Conference 80
Cocoa Marketing Board 7, 110, 112
Cocoa Strike / hold up Gold Coast 7, 8
Colonial Welfare and Development Act 55
Colour bar (in the UK) 5, 17, 29, 71-79, 81; in colonies 5, 73
Coloured Film Artists Association 20
Coloured Men's Institute 84
Coloured Workers Association (CWA) 111, 112

Come and See the Empire by the All Red Route 18
Communist Party (GB) 15
Compulsory / forced labour in colonies 49, 50, 51, 58, 59, 60, 61,-63, 64
Compulsory Native Labour Act (Rhodesias) 50, 64
Conference on African Peoples, Democracy and World Peace 16, 20
Conference of Labour Organisations, British Guiana 67
Congo 50
Congress Party (India) 10, 59
Conscientious Objectors' Tribunal 73
Conscription, to the military in colonies 34, 36, 59, 64
Constantine, Learie 75
Constitutional Reform Committee (Trinidad) 104
Convention People's Party 112
Corporal punishment of colonial troops 33, 34, 35, 79, 109
Cost of living, in colonies 62, 64, 66, 101, 102
Creech Jones, Arthur - see Jones, Arthur Creech
Critchlow, H.N. 84
Cripps, Sir Stafford 20, 59
Cross, Ulric, Squadron Leader 32, 36, 37, 42
Cummings, Ivor 72, 73, 74, 102
Cummings-John, Constance 8

D

Daily Comet 102
Dakar 33
Davies, H.O 109
Death rate, in military, see 'Casualty' - in tin mines, Nigeria 63
'Declaration to the Colonial People' Memorandum 109
Defence expenditure in India 41
Defence of India Act 10, 59
Desertions, from the military 34
De Gaulle, Charles 24

Dingwall, Eric J. 110
Domingo, W.A. 66
Dorman, Betty 109
Driberg, Tom, MP 74
Du Bois, W.E.B. 96, 108
Dunbar, Rudolph 80
Dutch East Indies 108
Dzifa, Kojo-ow 74

E

East Africa, 102
- price increases, unemployement 101
East Africa and Rhodesia 107
East African National Congress 103
Ebanks, John 32
Egypt 30, 32, 38
Ekpenyon, E.I. 72
Ellington, Ray 25
Emigrants from Britain 1
Empire Windrush 113
Emrys-Evans, Paul, MP 49
Erinpura, ss 32
Eritrea 24
Ethiopia 14, 33
European refugees in Africa 36

F

Fabian Colonial Bureau (FCB) 15, 60, 61, 62, 64, 81
Famine, in Bengal 60, 82
Federation of Indian Associations (UK) 107
Fiji Military Forces 26
Financial contributions from the colonies 49; from India 48; from Tanganyika 49; from West Africa 48; from the West Indies 48
Flogging – *see* 'Whipping'
Florent, Napoleon 74
Florent, Vivian 25
Food prices / rationing / shortages in the West Indies 66
Forsythe, Reginald 25
France 1, 19, 24, 38, 99
Freetown 8, 36

G

Gale, Percy 25
Gambia 49
Gandhi, Mohandas 10, 59, 60, 112
Gangulee, Professor 109
Garba-Jahumpa, Ibrahima 84, 109
Germany 1, 24, 98
Glasgow 17, 52, 82
Gold Coast (Ghana) 7, 8, 20, 50, 60, 63, 98, 101, 102, 112
- conscription 36
- US build air fields 34
Gold Coast Students Union (UK) 20, 111
Grant, Ulric 65-66
Greece 26, 49
Grigg, Sir J., Secretary of State for War 35

H

Hall, George, Under-Secretary of State for Colonies 42
Hawaii, Pearl Harbour 24, 90
Hill, Ken 109
Hindu Nationalist Party 60
Hiroshima 24, 98
Hitler, Adolf 24, 83, 90, 98, 106
Home Guard (UK) 76
Hong Kong 60
Horrabin, Frank 109
Hudson, Captain 77
Hudson, J.H. 19
Hull, Cordell (US Secretary of State) 90
Hyde, Ade 29

I

Imoudu, Michael 63
Imperial Hotel, London 75
Imperial Military Nursing Service 75
Imports, from Congo 50; from East Africa 49-50; from India 48, 50, 51, 52; from the Rhodesias 50, 51; from West Africa 48-50; from West Indies 49-50

Imprisonment of activists in colonies
6, 9, 10, 58, 59, 60, 62, 63, 64, 65-66,
80, 103, 112
Independent Labour Party (ILP) 6, 15,
17, 18, 19
India 2, 9-10, 19, 20, 24, 32, 38, 48,
59, 103, 108, 112
India and Burma Emergency Bill 59
India, British / US troops in 39, 48
- famine 60, 82
- financial contributions 48
- imports from 50, 51
- independence 103
- numbers killed/imprisoned for
'sedition'/striking 59, 103
- war 'casualty' numbers 32, 41
India League (UK) 13, 14, 17, 80, 82,
109
Indian Air Force 39
- Army 10, 38, 39
- Navy 39, 103
Indian National Congress (INC) 10,
38, 59
Indian seamen – see Lascar
Indian Women's Auxiliary 39
Indian Women's Naval Service 39
Indians' Victoria Crosses 40
Indians in Britain 82; in RAF 39;
Students' Union 112
Indo-China 108
Indonesia 109
International African Friends of
Abyssinia (IAFA) 14
International African Service Bureau
(IASB) 6, 8, 9, 13, 16, 19, 20, 77, 84,
102, 107
International Trade Union Committee
of Negro Workers (ITUC-NW) 14
International Transport Federation 52
Invader, Lord 67
Ipswich 76
Iraq 38, 49
Israel 34
Italy 24, 26, 34, 38
Itote, Waruhiu 101-102

J

Jacobs, Richard 38,
Jamaica 6, 41, 66, 92, 103, 113
Jamaica Reserve Regiment 38
James, C.L.R. 14
Japan 10, 24, 32, 90, 96, 98
Java / Javanese 9, 38
Jinnah, Muhammad Ali 10, 103, 112
Jones, Arthur Creech 20, 49, 61, 80,
109

K

Kaggia, Bildad 30
Kano, Mallam Aminu 111
Kaushal, Dr Baldev 72
Kenya 1, 35, 36, 49, 50, 51, 61, 64,
102-103,
Kenya African Union 103
Kenya Auxiliary Air Unit 35
- compulsory recruitment powers 64
- Defence Regulations 64
- Regiment (Whites only) 35
Kenyatta, Jomo 14, 106, 109
Khan, Noor Inayat 25-26
Khedive Ismail, ss 32
Kikuyu Central Organisation – members jailed 64
Killingray, David 31, 33
King, Amelia 25, 75
King's African Rifles (KAR) 30, 32,
33, 34, 101
King's Medal for Chiefs 34

L

Labour battalion / corps / units – see
Pioneer
Labour Party 82, 98
Labour shortage, in colonies 52, 54, 64
Lascar seamen 15, 52, 80
League Against Imperialism (LAI) 15
League of Coloured People (LCP) 6,
8, 13, 17, 20, 60, 62, 72, 73, 75, 76,
77, 78, 80, 81, 82- 83, 91- 92, 101,
107, 110, 111
League of Nations 99
Lebanon 34

Lend Lease Act 89, 112
Libya 24
Liverpool 5, 25, 52, 71, 76, 113
London Federation of Peace Councils
  17
Love, Geoff 25

M

Macmillan, Harold, Under Secretary of
  State for Colonies 61, 66
Madagascar 33
Mainwaring, William, MP 20
Makonnen, T. Ras 14, 15, 20, 106, 111
Malay Corps (South Africa) 35
Malaya 3, 38, 62, 99
Maldives 26
Malta 32, 34, 61
Manchester 107, 108
Manchuria (China) 24
'Manifesto on Africa in the Post-War
  World' 107
Manley, Norman 66
Mannin, Ethel 18
Maori troops 26
March, Dr. Leo 77
Marke, Ernest 112
Marshall Plan 112
May Day / International Workers' Day
  / Labour Day 106
McGuire, George 76
Medical Officers, African 60
Medical Service, in British military
  73, 77
'Memorandum on Legislation
  Involving Colour Discrimination' 99
Menon, Krishna 14, 15, 20, 80
Merchant Navy 15, 52, 62, 71
Merchant seamen, pay rates, pensions
  15, 29, 52, 80
Merchant vessels, sunk in Caribbean
  Sea 36
Middle East 27, 29, 30, 34, 36
Middle East Command, RAF 29
Military Academy, Sandhurst 79
  - Awards/Medals 26, 29, 31, 33, 37

- 'casualties' 32-3, 38, 41
- pay rates 29-31, 39, 78
Milliard, Dr Peter 106
Minh, Ho Chi 100
Mombasa 35
Monte Cassino 24, 39
Moody, Arundel 77
Moody, Dr Christine 77
Moody, Garth 77
Moody, Dr Harold (of the LCP) 20
Moody, Dr Harold 77, 81
Morgan, Dr. 66
Morris, Sam 111
Morrison, Herbert (Minister for
  Economic Affairs) 98
Moyne, Lord / Commission 7, 73
Murugiah, Mr. 111
Muslim League 10, 59

N

NAAFI 25
Nagasaki 24, 98
Nairobi, West African troops 35
National Association for the
  Advancement of Colored People
  (NAACP) 73, 96
National Council of Nigeria and
  Cameroons (NCNC) 63, 102, 110
National Maritime Board 52
National Union of Seamen 15, 52, 71
Native Military Corps, South Africa 35
'Native Races, the War and Peace
  Aims' Manifesto 80
Navigation Act, 1660 15
Negro Association 84
Negro Welfare Association (NWA) 6,
  13, 14, 17, 20
Negro Welfare Centre 84
Negro Worker 8
Nehru, Jawaharlal 10, 17, 18, 59, 60,
  80, 103, 112
New African, The 109
Newfoundland 41
New Zealand 1, 26, 32

Ngarimu, Te Moananui-a-Kiwa,
  Platoon Leader 25, 26
Nigeria 7, 8, 36, 48-51, 60- 63, 82,
  102, 106, 108, 110, 111, 112
Nigerian Union (UK) 111
Nimbkar, R. S. 20
Nkrumah, Kwame 109, 110, 111, 112
Noel-Baker, Philip, MP 82
North Africa 26, 29, 33, 34, 35, 36, 38,
  49

O

Oil 3, 6, 41
  - from Trinidad 6, 49, 50
Ojiako, Mr. 111
Orissa, famine 60
Otubisin, Miss 111
Orizu, Nwafor 92

P

Padmore, George 8, 14, 16, 17, 20, 41,
  76, 79, 91, 97, 106, 109
Pakistan 103, 112
Palestine 19
Pan-Africa 112
Pan-African Conference/Congress,
  1945 107-108
Pan-African Federation 106, 108, 110,
  111
Paris Peace Conference 99, 100
Pay-rates, military 29-31, 39, 78
'Peace and Empire' Conference 17
Pearl Harbour 24, 90
Pensions, gratuities, for the military /
  merchant seamen 30, 31, 47, 52
People's National Party (PNP), Jamaica
  66, 92
Perham, Margery 2
Phelps Stokes Fund 83
Pioneer (colonial labour) Corps 25, 28,
  29, 31, 32, 34, 64, 71
Polish refugees in Africa 36, 64
Port Elizabeth 9
Prescott, Captain, MP 31
Price, George C. 77
Princess Tsahai 20

Prisoners-of-War (POW) 32, 38, 41
Propaganda, by Britain in colonies 29
Pujji, Mahinder Singh, Squadron
  Leader 39

Q

Quit India Movement 10, 38, 59, 82

R

Race Relations and The Schools (by
  LCP) 83
Racial discrimination/segregation in
  the colonies 7-9, 26, 63-64, 67, 80,
  99, 102, 108
  - in the military/RN/RAF 10, 16-17,
    24, 29-31, 35, 73, 77-79 , 35, 73,
    77-79
  - in the UK 2, 5, 15, 16, 37, 53, 58,
    71-76, 80-81, 98-99
Racial Pride and Prejudice 110
Railway Employees Union, Jamaica
  66, 103
Ransome-Kuti, Funmilayo 106, 110
Recruitment (free and forced) for the
  military 28-39, 58, 64; Recruitment
  Regulations 77, 78
  - for the merchant marine 71
  - of workers 50, 51, 52, 53, 61-63,
    64, 65
Refugees, from Europe in Africa 64
Rhodesia 1, 7, 51, 64
Rhodesia, North (Zambia) 34, 50, 61,
  63-64
Rhodesia, South (Zimbabwe) 34, 63
Ridley, F.A. 6
Riley, Benjamin, MP 34
Riot, Liverpool, anti-Black 113
Roosevelt, President Franklin Delano
  60, 88-90
Royal Air Force (RAF) 6, 8, 36, 37,
  48, 49, 54, 73
  - colonials / 'Black' Britons in 25,
    29, 39, 65 , 76, 77, 78
Royal Indian Navy 39, 48, 78, 103
Royal Naval Voluntary Reserve
  (RNVR) 33, 37

Royal Navy 6, 33, 35, 36, 54, 73, 77,
    78, 79
    - South Atlantic Command 36
Royal West African Frontier Force
    (RWAFF) 32, 33, 34, 35, 101, 110

S

Salisbury, Bishop of 74
Sandhurst, Royal Military Academy
    35
Scottish Peace Council 18
Security Council, UNO 96
Seditious Ordinance, Sierra Leone 9;
    West Indies 67
Shenbanjo, Akin 29
Sicily 34
Sierra Leone 8, 9, 36, 49, 61, 62, 101
Sierra Leone Union (UK) 111
Singapore 10, 39, 48
Smuts, General Jan 9, 82, 99
Socialist International 17
Solanke, Ladipo 14
Somalia 24, 33
Sorensen, Reginald, MP 35, 79, 80,
    109
South Africa 1, 9, 32, 33, 34, 35,
    63-64, 82, 99
    - total segregation 35
    - war casualty numbers 32
South-West Africa 24
South Atlantic Command (RN) 36
South Shields, Arab Community in 71
South-West Africa 24
Soviet Union – *see* USSR
Special Operations Executive (SOE) 26
Stanley, Col. Oliver, Colonial Secretary
    31, 34, 37, 55, 62
St.Lucia 6, 36, 41; Castries 36
Strikes / protests – in colonies 6, 8, 9,
    51, 60, 62, 63, 64, 66, 93, 102, 103,
    108
    - forbidden in colonies 58, 63; 66,
    103
    - by colonial seamen in UK 52, 80
Subject People's Conference 107

Sukanaivalu, Sefanaia, Crpl. 26
Swaziland 9
Syria 38, 49

T

Tanganyika (Tanzania) 24, 49, 50, 60,
    61, 64
Tanganyikan Field Battery 34
Taussig, Charles 92
Thompson, Dudley, Flight Lt. 7
Thompson, Leslie 25
Togoland 24
Torres Strait Regiment 26
Trade unions, discrimination by (UK)
    53
    - forbidden in colonies 58, 63, 67
Trinidad 6, 36, 41, 49, 50, 65, 66, 67,
    103- 104; Port-of-Spain 36, 65
Trinidad Royal Naval Reserve 38
Trusteeship Council 97, 99
Tsahai, Princess 20
Tunisia 26

U

U-boats in Caribbean Sea 36
Uganda 36, 64
Unemployment, Gold Coast 102;
    Nigeria 102; Sierra Leone 101; West
    Indies 66, 103
UK, debt to India 48
United Gold Coast Convention
    (UGCC) 102, 112
United Nations Organisation (UNO)
    82, 83, 84, 88, 96-97, 99, 102, 107,
    109, 110
United Socialist movement 17
USA, and British colonies 41-42,
    88-94, 107, 112-113
    - Air Transport Command 36
    - military bases in West Indies 36,
      41, 65, 67; in West Africa 36; in
      India 39
    - segregation policy 73, 74
    - West Indian workers in 66, 71
Universal suffrage granted to West
    Indian colonies 104

Usmani, Mr. 111
USSR / Russia 88, 96, 97

V

Vichy 24, 33
Villard, Henry (US State Dept.) 91

W

Wachuku, Jaja 109
Wakefield, Sir Wavell, MP 31
Wallace-Johnson, I.T.A. 8, 9, 14, 62, 106, 109
War Bonus, for seamen 52, 80
War 'casualty rates' 32-3, 38, 41
Ward, Arnold 14
Waters, Leonard, Flight Sgt. 25, 26
Weekes, George 73
Welles, Sumner 93
West Africa / Africans 62-63; 82, 101, 102, 109, 110
West Africa, price increases / unemployment 101, 102
 - US troops in 36
West African financial contributions 48
 - Medical Corps / Division 33
 - military / troops 29, 33-35, 78, 101, 110; medals won 32
 - women in Air Services 33
West African National Secretariat (WANS) 109- 110, 111, 112
West African Parliamentary Committee 80
West African seamen 16
West Africa's sterling assets, post-war 98
West African Pilot 82, 112; banned 102
West African Students' Union (WASU) 8, 13, 14, 72, 77, 80, 82, 91, 102, 110, 111
West African Youth League 8
West India Regiment 11, 65
West Indian military 5, 28; Caribbean Regiment 30, 36, 37; 'casualty' rates 38; racial discrimination 30
 - financial contributions 48

- women in ATS (in UK) 37, 71
- workers in the USA 54, 103; in Britain 52
West Indian Students' Union 111
West Indians in RAF 36, 37, 65, 78
West Indies 5-6, 7, 17, 20, 24, 28, 36, 42, 62, 66, 67, 92, 99, 103-104
 - food rationing / shortage 66
 - imports from 49-50
 - land exchanged for US destroyers 41
 - strikes 103
 - U-boats 36
 - USA military bases 36, 41, 67
 - workers recruited by Britain 52-54, 65
Whipping of African soldiers 34, 78, 79, 109
Williams, Eric 104
Willkie, Wendell 90
Women's Auxiliary Air Force (WAAF) 25-26
Women's Auxiliary Army Corps (US) 76
Women's Land Army 25, 75
Woodburn, Arthur, MP 77
Workers' Exhibition 18
World Federation of Trade Unions 84, 99, 106
World War I, colonial troops 2

Y

Young, Arthur 25

Z

Zanzibar 61